Achieving Your
PTLLS Award

Achieving Your PTLLS Award

A Practical Guide to Successful Teaching in the Lifelong Learning Sector

Mary Francis and Jim Gould

Los Angeles | London | New Delhi
Singapore | Washington DC

First published 2009

Reprinted 2009, 2010, 2011

SAGE Publications Ltd
1 Oliver's Yard
55 City Road
London EC1Y 1SP

SAGE Publications Inc.
2455 Teller Road
Thousand Oaks, California 91320

SAGE Publications India Pvt Ltd
B 1/I 1 Mohan Cooperative Industrial Area
Mathura Road
New Delhi 110 044

SAGE Publications Asia-Pacific Pte Ltd
33 Pekin Street #02-01
Far East Square
Singapore 048763

Library of Congress Control Number: 2008934763

British Library Cataloguing in Publication data

A catalogue record for this book is available from the British Library

ISBN 978-1-84787-916-5
ISBN 978-1-84787-917-2 (pbk)

Typeset by C&M Digitals (P) Ltd., Chennai, India
Printed in Great Britain by CPI Antony Rowe, Chippenham, Wiltshire
Printed on paper from sustainable resources

Contents

Acknowledgements

The authors would like to thank the following:
Caroline Allen, Dave Baber, Suzanne Dunsmore, Sara Halsey, Pip Kings, Kieran Allen Lowe, Pauline Mason, Stephen Norris, Esther Schmitz, Yvette Raikes and Allan Woods.

Drawings are by Lisa Bailey.

Introduction: Welcome to Achieving your PTLLS Award!

There are some questions you will want answered as you begin to use this book.

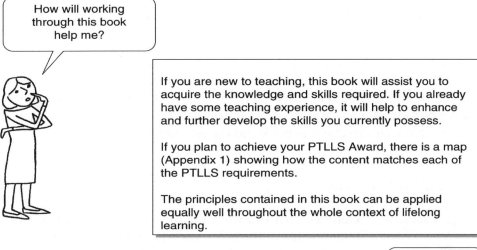

How will working through this book help me?

If you are new to teaching, this book will assist you to acquire the knowledge and skills required. If you already have some teaching experience, it will help to enhance and further develop the skills you currently possess.

If you plan to achieve your PTLLS Award, there is a map (Appendix 1) showing how the content matches each of the PTLLS requirements.

The principles contained in this book can be applied equally well throughout the whole context of lifelong learning.

What sort of information is contained in the book?

This book covers:
- The role of the teacher
- Planning systematically for teaching
- Inclusive approaches to learning
- Methods for different subject areas
- Motivating and managing learners
- Assessment and evaluation techniques
- Planning a microteaching session

In short, all you need to know to complete a PTLLS course and a little bit more!

How will this help to develop my skills?

In each section you will find a number of activities.
By completing these, you will see how the information applies to your own particular situation.

Features of the book

Each chapter of this book has the following features:

- An overview and rationale so that you have a complete picture of each chapter's content and understand its intended outcomes, structure and importance.
- A mix of short exercises and questions to encourage you to reflect upon the issues. This will be either from the perspective of your own experience, if you are currently in a teaching role, or as areas for consideration if you are a prospective rather than a practising teacher.
- Space for you to record your reflections.
- Discussion of appropriate/expected responses, to provide you with feedback.
- At the end of each chapter, a summary of the main learning points covered.
- Suggested websites and further reading, annotated to give you a brief overview of the nature and level of the book and the relevant areas to consult.

Symbols you will meet

Chapter overview

Outlines what you will work through in this chapter. The bullet points in the box show what you will achieve after completing the chapter.

Activity

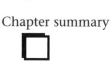

Read and apply what you have read to your own teaching situation. Record your responses in the box.

Chapter summary

When you reach the chapter summary box this is an opportunity for you to make sure you have taken in all the main points made so far before going on to the next chapter.

Further reading

Suggested books and, where appropriate, websites related to the content of the particular chapter which will enable you to further develop your thinking.

Useful websites

At the end of the book you will find:

- Appendices, including example session plans
- A glossary explaining the main terms used in the text

1

Becoming a professional in the lifelong learning sector – roles, responsibilities and boundaries

Chapter overview

When you have worked through this chapter on becoming a professional you will be able to:

- **Describe what is meant by the lifelong learning sector**
- **Explain the current drive towards professionalism in the lifelong learning sector and its implications for those working in it**
- **Review the roles, responsibilities and boundaries of professionals in the sector**
- **Identify other points of referral to meet the potential needs of learners**
- **Recognise key aspects of relevant current legislative requirements and codes of practice relevant to your own context**

Teaching in the lifelong learning sector

If you are reading this book we expect that you are preparing to teach in the lifelong learning sector and may well be interested in gaining the PTLLS Award.

So what does this lifelong learning sector look like? It is a sector that covers all publicly funded post-16 education outside universities; this takes place in a wide range of institutions including Further Education (FE) colleges, adult and community education, private training providers of work-based learning, libraries, archives and information services and prisons. Some interesting facts about the lifelong learning sector include:

1   Three-quarters of learners are 19+ and part-time
2   There are more 16 – 19 year olds in colleges of FE than in sixth forms in secondary schools
3   Learners range from those who cannot read, write or communicate to those at post-degree level
4   There are more students in FE colleges than in universities
5   One in five adults are currently learning, with 42% of adults having participated in some learning activity during the past three years
6   Over £19 billion was spent on this sector in 2008
7   The majority of the workforce is female
8   Part-time teaching staff in FE outnumber full-time teaching staff by almost 2:1

Is this a picture that you recognise? The role of a professional in the lifelong learning sector is extremely diverse; you may be called a lecturer, a tutor, a trainer, an instructor, an assessor, a work-based learning or an apprentice supervisor, a learning manager or a prison education officer. Some of you may have gained skills and experience through another trade or profession, for example as an engineer, hairdresser or bricklayer. What you are likely to have in common is that you will all have a teaching or training function with learners aged 16 and above. For the purpose of this book we will use the term 'teacher' generically to apply to all these various roles and 'learner' to apply to those who you may also call students, pupils or apprentices.

Professional teachers in the lifelong learning sector also share in the common purpose of serving the needs of learners, employers and the community. They face the challenges of working in a context which is diverse and rapidly changing. The past decade has seen significant change for the sector; the next decade will be marked by the emergence of new funding bodies taking over from the Learning and Skills Council and local authorities taking on enhanced responsibilities for 14–19 planning and funding.

The government is convinced that the lifelong learning sector has never been more crucial in raising the overall level of skills and ensuring the UK remains competitive in the world economy. You will be expected to play a role in helping to meet current key targets; these include ensuring all adults are functionally literate and numerate, all 19 year olds have a Level 2 or equivalent (5 GCSEs at Grade A* to C) and that learners are qualified to meet vital skills shortages. It is expected that 50% of 18–30 year olds will progress to university by 2010. In order to meet these targets more young people will need to remain in education and training and more will need to succeed; lifelong learning professionals are accountable for such performance.

The move towards Qualified Teacher status – Learning and Skills

A new framework of teacher qualifications for the Learning and Skills sector was introduced in England in September 2007. From now on all teachers, trainers and tutors offered jobs in colleges and other publicly funded organisations will need to have an appropriate teaching qualification. This followed various reports indicating that some learners were not being taught by properly qualified and experienced staff. The government sees a professional workforce as a key element in realising its aim to raise standards, to get rid of poor performance in colleges and to enable colleges to respond more effectively to employers' needs.

If you are preparing to teach in the lifelong learning sector it is therefore likely that you will take a qualification that is part of the Qualified Teacher – Learning and Skills (QTLS) framework. The first qualification is called Preparing to Teach in the Lifelong Learning Sector (PTLLS), the 'threshold licence to teach' for all new teachers in the FE sector. This book focuses on helping you to achieve the PTLLS Award.

The success of learners depends, to a great extent, on the commitment and skills of the teaching staff. Setting PTLLS as the basic minimum standard for all new entrants to the profession should ensure all students in the lifelong learning sector are taught by teachers and trainers who are both experienced in their subject and skilled in teaching.

Roles and responsibilities of teachers in the lifelong learning sector

In this section we will begin to consider your work in the lifelong learning sector. As we have seen above, it is a much more diverse sector than the school sector. We will focus on the following two questions:

1 What roles are you expected to fulfil?
2 What are the specific responsibilities and boundaries associated with these roles?

When we talk about a 'role' most people instantly think of playing a part, or acting in some capacity. A role involves some idea of expected behaviour associated with a position. You will have expectations of the learners or students that you will teach, train, assess or tutor. These may include an expectation that they will study and undergo assessments.

When we look at the role of a teacher, trainer, assessor or tutor we find that there is a body of agreed expectations associated with these roles.

 Activity 1.1

What do you expect someone who is a lecturer, teacher, trainer, assessor or tutor in the lifelong learning sector to do?

Now look at these three examples of a typical day of a lifelong learning professional:

Case study 1: Assessor in the workplace

Travel to employer premises

Review a portfolio

Meet a NVQ candidate and check underpinning knowledge

Discuss learner progress with another assessor

Attend an internal verification meeting

Lunch

Identify key skills needs of a candidate

Candidate is having problems gaining experience to demonstrate their competence. Talk to workplace supervisor

Fill out travel expenses claim form

Check the latest sector skills council briefing

Case study 2: FE lecturer

Arrive at college, check pigeon-hole

Check preparation for first lesson, last-minute photocopying

Give first part of lesson

Break – check college emails

Give second part of lesson

Lesson finished – deal with related administration

Give new part-time colleague advice on initial assessment

Get lunch from canteen

Discuss discipline problem with a colleague

Answer two telephone calls relating to course enquiries

Eat (now cold) lunch

Help a tutee with personal statement and UCAS form

Accept sick note from tutee, and mark register/tutorial notes

Scan internal memos

Prepare mark sheet for exam

Teach lesson

Mark assignments ready for tutorial

Review learner minimum grade expectations on college intranet

Give tutorial

Share resources with colleague

Case study 3: Voluntary sector worker

Organise a room for a briefing session with volunteer tutors

Plan an introductory session

Take the register

Conduct an ice-breaker

Explain the volunteer role

Discuss volunteer placements

Complete learner records

Telephone a volunteer who missed the session

Meet a volunteer who is having problems relating to an autistic learner

Fill out an application for funding for a future course

Check charity website for publicity on Volunteer Training programme

Activity 1.2

What do these three roles have in common?

The first thing that will probably strike you is that a lot of time is spent in activities that are not directly concerned with imparting knowledge or skills. You will probably come to the conclusion that the role of a teacher has many sub-roles and so equally do other roles in the lifelong learning sector.

These may include any or all of the following:

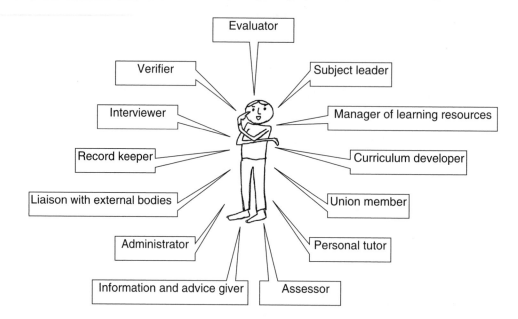

Evaluator
Verifier
Subject leader
Interviewer
Manager of learning resources
Record keeper
Curriculum developer
Liaison with external bodies
Union member
Administrator
Personal tutor
Information and advice giver
Assessor

Activity 1.3

Thinking of your own context, what roles do you expect to play? Looking at the sub-roles we have identified, tick any you think you will have. If any have been overlooked, add these to the list.

Which of these do you consider to be your core 'professional' roles?

With each of these sub-roles come associated responsibilities; these will be shaped by national legislation (for example, health and safety), institutional requirements (for example, the responsibility to ensure a policy on lateness is consistently carried out) and situational requirements (for example, responsibility to ensure no eating or drinking in a computer room). These associated responsibilities imply dependability, conscientiousness and trustworthiness on the part of the teacher.

A key responsibility of a teacher in the lifelong learning sector, for example, is the checking and reporting of learner attendance and achievement. This is necessary for monitoring progress of learners and in order for the organisation to report accurately to funding and inspection bodies. Largely, however, the responsibilities of a lifelong learning professional involve 'doing a proper job' by, for example:

- Treating all learners fairly and with equal respect (Equality and diversity)
- Giving learners the opportunity to participate on equal terms and with an equal expectation of success (Equality)
- Engaging all learners involving all learners in relevant activities (Inclusion)
- Acknowledging and celebrating the diversity in a group of learners (Differentiation)
- Planning to meet the needs and styles of individual learners (Personalisation)
- Keeping up to date with subject developments
- Being well prepared
- Returning marked work in a reasonable time

Current legislative requirements

The lifelong learning professional also has responsibilities to ensure that current legislative requirements are met.

Whilst some legislation and codes of practice are at least in part subject-related, there is a considerable body of legislation that applies within the lifelong learning sector as a whole. 'Every Child Matters: Change for Children' (ECM) and the related provisions in the Children Act 2004 provide an example of this. In the wake of the inquiry into the death of Victoria Climbié (2003), the government sought a strategy that would promote the well-being of children and young people aged 0–19. It aimed to ensure that agencies and institutions that provide services for children would work together in new ways to avoid a repetition of such tragedies. The five outcomes sought by ECM are:

- Be healthy
- Stay safe
- Enjoy and achieve
- Make a positive contribution
- Achieve economic well-being

Although 'child' figures in the title, all institutions within the lifelong learning sector that deal with learners up to the age of 19 have to comply with ECM and it is one of the criteria against which the inspectorate Ofsted judges the performance of FE colleges. Allied to this is the Protection of Children Act 1999 whereby teachers who come into contact with children or vulnerable adults are subject to the Enhanced Disclosure check by the Criminal Records Bureau (CRB).

These are merely two examples of legislation to be aware of. The list below provides other examples:

1 Legislation relating to **Health and Safety** – the responsibility to provide a safe environment, both physical and psychological:

   - Health & Safety at Work Act 1974
   - Manual Handling Operations Regulations 1992
   - RIDDOR – Reporting of Injuries, Diseases and Dangerous Occurrences Regulations 1995
   - Management of the Health & Safety at Work Act 1999
   - COSHH – Control of Substances Hazardous to Health Regulations 2002

2 Legislation relating to **Disability** – the responsibility to make 'reasonable adjustments' for learners:

   - DDA – Disability and Discrimination Act 1995
   - DDA Part 4 Code of Practice 1995
   - SENDA – Special Educational Needs and Disability Act 2001

3 Legislation relating to **Human Rights** – including the responsibility to ensure equality on the basis of gender/ethnicity/disability/age/religion/ sexual orientation:

   - Sex Discrimination Act 1975
   - Race Relations Act 1976 (amended 2000)
   - Human Rights Act 1998
   - Equality Act 2006

In more general terms, legislation such as The Copyright Design and Patents Act 1988 and The Data Protection Act 1998 also impact on working life and habits within the sector. In your role in lifelong learning you will therefore need to adhere to legislation outlined above and have particular awareness of any legislative responsibilities relevant to the teaching of your subject.

Establishing professional and personal boundaries

If we perform the roles required of us, with the associated responsibilities, we will exemplify what we call 'professionalism' in the lifelong learning sector. Professionalism requires us to maintain appropriate standards and fulfil our responsibilities to learners, institutions and colleagues.

In April 2008, a Code of Professional Practice was introduced covering the activities of teachers in the Lifelong Learning Sector. The Institute for Learning (IfL) is responsible for enforcing the code which is based around the six areas of:

- Professional integrity
- Respect for others
- Care of learners
- Continuing professional development
- Disclosure of criminal offence
- Responsibility towards IfI

Full details can be found at www.ifl.ac.uk/services/docs/1269/CodeofProfessional Practice.pdf

Teachers in the lifelong learning sector work with a range of other professionals and support staff. The way in which we perform our role can be influenced by others: for example, learners or line managers. Together these other roles make up your role set, the group with whom you relate in your role as a teacher and who can have an impact on how you act as a teacher.

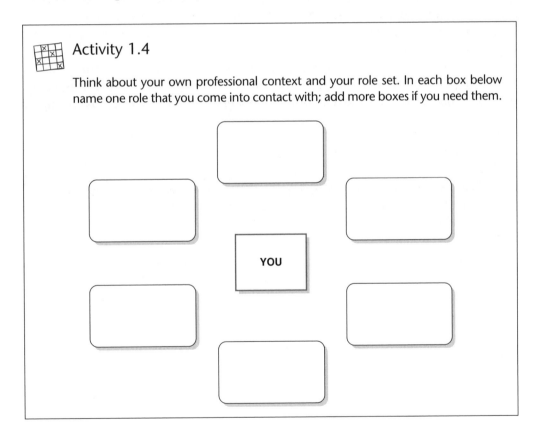

Activity 1.4

Think about your own professional context and your role set. In each box below name one role that you come into contact with; add more boxes if you need them.

YOU

The role set that you drew up above is particular to your own situation. It may have included management, support staff – librarians, technicians, reprographic staff – administrators, finance, counsellors, union representatives and governors. Those who make up your role set can often place conflicting demands on you as a teacher, pulling you in different directions; this is known as role strain.

Activity 1.5

If you look at your role set above, what two roles might expect you to act in two different ways? What kind of role strain might develop?

Some tutors in adult and community education find considerable strain results from the caretaker imposing demands about room layout and getting students out of the class promptly at the end of the evening. This may make it difficult for you to meet expectations from your line manager that you will resolve an issue with an individual learner when you still need five minutes to find a way forward.

Because individuals with whom you work may place what you consider to be unacceptable demands on you, it is necessary to have a clear idea as to how you see your role and what you should do in order to fulfil it. In part, this requires the setting of professional and personal boundaries and is an important aspect of professionalism. In this context a boundary is a limit on the extent of involvement.

 Activity 1.6

If a learner presents the following issue, do you consider it falls within your role and responsibilities as a teacher in the lifelong learning sector? If not, to whom could you refer this issue? Fill out the columns below:

Learner Issue	Yes/No	Referral to?
Anxiety		
Abortion		
Abuse		
Bereavement		
Bullying		
Career issues		
Diet		
Depression		
Drug/alcohol problems		
Failing		

Learner Issue	Yes/No	Referral to?
Family problems		
Grant problems		
Harassment		
Illness		
Marital breakdown		
Prolonged absence		
Racial conflict or tensions		
Stress		
Study skills		

Making use of internal and external support

In Activity 1.6 you will have identified areas that you consider to be outside your professional boundaries. Either you think it is inappropriate to deal with these or feel that you do not have the necessary skills or expertise. Support from someone else will be needed and it is important that you can identify who this might be. Institutions have a range of support systems and you should check your organisational structure chart and see what is available internally to supplement your work with learners.

 Activity 1.7

Which of the following support roles does your own institution provide?

- A counsellor
- Financial advice
- Career guidance
- Leisure activities
- A tutorial system
- Crèche facilities
- Additional Learning Support
- A learning resource centre

Learners can present a variety of problems which may prevent them from making progress with their studies or life plans. You will be better able to help them if you are fully aware of internal and external support mechanisms which are available to them.

In this chapter we have focused on your role as a professional in the lifelong learning sector. In the following chapters we will explore different aspects of this role and associated responsibilities, starting with the responsibility as a teacher to create an appropriate environment in which learning can take place.

▢ Chapter summary

The main points covered in this chapter are:

✓ Lifelong learning encompasses a range of different types of provision
✓ The role of the teacher in the lifelong learning sector is not confined to imparting knowledge and skills but covers a multiplicity of different tasks
✓ Roles are accompanied by responsibilities and these contribute to the adoption of a professional approach to work in the lifelong learning sector
✓ A professional approach involves being aware of and upholding current legislation and codes of practice
✓ The relationship between your role and that of others with whom you work may sometimes lead to tensions or 'role strain'
✓ Teachers in the lifelong learning sector need to be aware of both professional boundaries and their own personal limitations, knowing when and to whom to refer learners for further support

---

📖 Further reading

Coles, A. (2004) *Teaching in Post – Compulsory Education: Policy Practice and Values.* London: David Fulton Publishers.
Chapter 3 of this book directly addresses the role of the post-compulsory teacher, outlining a wide variety of sub-roles with appropriate background.

Tummons, J. (2007) *Becoming a Professional Tutor in the Lifelong Learning Sector.* Exeter: Learning Matters.
Chapter 2 examines the purpose of the lifelong sector and how this impacts upon the professional role, with particular reference to accountability. Chapter 3 looks at the reasons behind codes of practice and how they impact upon role.

🖱 Useful websites

Lifelong Learning UK
   www.lluk.org
Further Education Teacher's Qualifications
   www.dius.gov.uk/publications/guide2007no2264.pdf
   www.opsi.gov.uk/si/si2007/em/uksiem_20072264_en.pdf
Role of FE teacher
   www.learndirect-advice.co.uk/helpwithyourcareer/jobprofiles/profiles/profile405/
Institute for Learning (IfL)
   www.ifl.ac.uk

For websites related to equality and diversity, see end of Chapter 5.

2

Establishing a positive environment

Chapter overview

When you have worked through this chapter on the environment you will be able to:

- Identify the three aspects of the learning environment and how to manage these to optimise learning
- Recognise the effects of the environment on patterns of communication
- State the need for ground rules and identify appropriate ways of setting these
- List different methods of 'breaking the ice'
- Describe a model of the communication process and the characteristics of effective verbal and non-verbal communication
- Identify potential barriers to communication and how to overcome these

In the next few chapters we will be looking at our learners and the decisions that have to be made in planning and delivering teaching sessions. In a sense it is like a musician preparing for a concert. The music has been chosen and practised until it can be played without mistakes. Is this enough, however, to make the concert a success?

Our musician will also be thinking about the best way to set out the concert hall. Is the audience to dance, or sit and listen? This will affect issues such as whether seating is provided, whether only the stage will be lit or the whole hall. Will there in fact be a stage? If the musician wishes the audience to join in, it may be better to sit at the same level or even in the middle of the audience.

How will our musician create a relationship or rapport with the audience; will he or she talk to them and if so, how? All of these concerns are to do with creating an appropriate environment within which the performance will take place. We have to address similar issues in any form of teaching in which we engage.

One way we can define teaching is:

The teacher creates the optimum environment in which people can learn.

What do we mean when we use the term 'environment' in this context? One interpretation suggests the teaching environment has three aspects:

1   The **physical** environment
2   The **social** environment
3   The **learning** environment

Although we have listed these separately, in reality each has an effect on the other and each is equally important in the planning of any teaching that we undertake.

The **learning** environment is concerned with giving the session a sense of purpose and direction. In Chapter 4 we will look at how we might achieve this through the way in which we systematically plan teaching sessions and so we will focus here on the other two aspects of the teaching environment.

The **physical environment** is about the surroundings within which teaching takes place, while the **social environment** concerns how you put your learners at ease and establish rapport with them.

 Activity 2.1

What do you think makes a good physical environment for learning?

What do you think makes a good social environment for learning?

Physical environment

One aspect of this environment is the actual physical conditions under which teaching takes place. Is the room too hot, too stuffy? Is it too bright or too dark for the method you plan to use?

Another aspect of the physical environment is to do with the arrangement of the furniture and resources. This is affected by two related factors:

- The methods we are using
- The kind of interaction we wish to take place

Different methods and activities will require teachers and learners to take on different roles, which in turn will require different types of interaction.

Do we want learners to take a passive role where they mainly listen and perhaps take notes? Alternatively, are we looking for them to take a more active role, where they contribute, join in and discuss? Do we wish attention to be focused more on learners and their performance? Answers to these questions will influence the type of communication we will wish to encourage. This in turn will influence the way in which we organise the physical environment in which our teaching will take place.

We can classify communication in a number of different ways. These are:

One-way
We talk to the learners who listen and do not contribute unless specifically asked. Attention is focused on us and on the resource we are presenting. This would be appropriate in any form of teaching in which we present information in a logical sequence.

Two-way
We talk to the learners who listen, but they will also ask questions and will be encouraged to make contributions of their own, although we would normally expect them to do this through us. A more interactive approach is sought and attention needs to be focused on whoever is speaking at the time.

Several-ways
Everyone makes contributions and asks questions, addressing the group as a whole. This situation might arise when we are having a discussion with learners, who are expressing ideas and opinions. Alternatively, if learners are seeking information for themselves, they may be doing this in small groups involving several-way communication.

Room layout

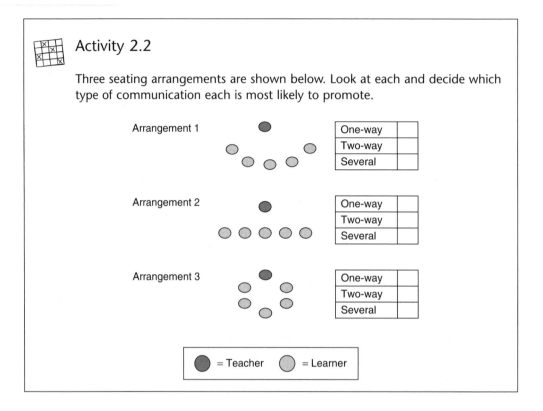

Activity 2.2

Three seating arrangements are shown below. Look at each and decide which type of communication each is most likely to promote.

For solution, see page 35.

Adding desks or tables also makes a difference. Consider the layout below:

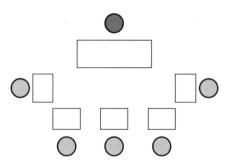

You can see that tables create a barrier; this results in a more formal learning situation. This layout tends to cut down the chances of two-way and several-ways communication. Tables also constitute a 'safety barrier', however, (as well as providing a surface for writing) and learners may well feel exposed by their absence.

The way we set up the environment, whether we include tables and chairs, even whether we, as teachers, sit or stand, makes a difference to where attention is focused. These factors can either encourage or inhibit different patterns of communication. Some arrangements will give a 'formal' feel to the session, others a more 'informal' or relaxed feel in which the learners may feel more at ease. The key factor is the amount of eye contact that can be made.

The physical environment, however, is not the only factor that determines the atmosphere or climate within which the session takes place. To see what else plays a part we must now look to the social environment.

Social environment

Generally, we learn best when we are relaxed and feel comfortable with what we are experiencing in the teaching environment – when we feel secure and largely free from anxiety. It is part of our role as teachers to establish such a climate for learners, but how is this achieved? There is no simple answer as a combination of different factors is involved.

To start thinking about these, consider all of the factors that would make you feel **uncomfortable** in your learning. It may help to think back to occasions when you have been taught yourself and, in some way, found it to be an unpleasant or uncomfortable experience.

Activity 2.3

Things that make me uncomfortable in my learning include:

Some of the factors you have listed above will be related to the teaching itself and we will address these in later chapters. Some will be more to do with how you feel in the learning environment, whereas others will be to do with the teacher and their attitudes and actions. How do your thoughts compare with the lists below?

To do with how learners feel

- Lack of confidence in own ability
- Not valued or respected
- Lack of motivation

- Unsure of other learners
- Not listened to
- It's a test or a threat

To do with the teacher's attitudes and actions

- Unenthusiastic teachers
- Disorganised or badly prepared teachers
- Teachers who are sarcastic or impatient with learners
- Teaching is conducted in a competitive atmosphere
- Teachers who patronise learners
- Teachers who put learners 'on the spot'
- Teachers who make premature judgements about learners
- Teachers who show little interest in their learners or do not recognise learners as individuals
- Teachers who use material that does not suit the learners

In your own teaching sessions you will want to establish a climate very different from that above. A positive social climate is unlikely to be achieved immediately, but is built up gradually. It is something that we need to work towards from when we first meet learners.

The first meeting between the teacher and the learner or learners is a significant time in establishing the sort of climate that is conducive to learning. One of the major aims of the first session is to reduce anxiety levels and to begin to establish some form of relationship or rapport between the teacher and learners and between the different learners themselves.

First impressions

We don't get a second chance to make a first impression, so the impression we create both individually and as an institution needs to be positive.

Institutions often have induction policies which are designed to ensure that all learners have as smooth a transition as possible into their new programmes of study and the culture and expectations of the institution.

 Activity 2.4

What do you think should be included in an induction programme?

A typical induction programme will include:

- Finding your way about the site
- Introduction to staff
- Introduction to any services such as learning resource centre, information, advice and guidance (IAG), counselling, welfare
- Health and Safety information
- Learning Agreements
- Developing your Individual Learning Plan (ILP)
- Policies, for example Complaints, Equality and Diversity

When we first meet learners, some of the things they will notice about us are:

- Appearance – are we suitably dressed?
- Bearing – do we appear confident, open and friendly?
- Level of preparation – are we organised, structured and well prepared?

How we 'measure up' in these areas will, at least in the first instance, determine how learners will react to us and how much confidence they will have in our ability to provide them with the sort of teaching they would want and expect.

How we dress will be a matter of personal preference, but whatever we wear, it should be appropriate to the type of teaching we will be doing. If it is a workshop environment, for instance, a white coat or overalls may be appropriate. A tracksuit is appropriate for sports coaching. In any event we should be dressed so that the learners feel we have made some effort with our appearance on their behalf.

Similarly with preparation, having the appropriate paperwork and teaching resources to hand shows we have put thought into the teaching that is to be received. This is borne out by a confident introduction and a session that flows smoothly from one section to the next.

Body language also plays its part: we should maintain good eye contact, adopt an open posture and, possibly most important of all **SMILE** and **MEAN IT!**

Openings

Our initial contact with learners can be used to dispel many of the fears and anxieties that may exist. Our manner is an important factor in this, so it helps to be welcoming and to learn and use names at the earliest opportunity. In any opening remarks, we are aiming to establish our credibility as teachers. This can be achieved by referring to our experience and qualifications. We do not wish to become unapproachable, so care should be taken not to overdo this. We are aiming to reassure learners of our capabilities, not scare them off.

At this stage we would also tell them a little about the course:

- What they might expect from it
- The ground that will be covered
- The activities they will engage in

- Expectations of workload
- Any work-related activities
- How progress will be checked
- What their part in it will be

By doing this we are aiming to take the 'fear of the unknown' out of the teaching so that learners will feel reassured and more relaxed in their learning. A feeling of trust and confidentiality must be conveyed.

Ground rules

You may at this stage also wish to introduce some ground rules relating to the way you are to function together as a group. Theories of group development suggest that groups form in a series of stages. The first stage involves the coming together of the members of the potential group. This is followed by a 'jostling for position' before 'norms', or expectations of behaviour, from those in the group, begin to emerge. It is only after this last stage that the group begins to function as a working unit. These stages are summarised as forming, storming, norming and performing (Tuckmann, 1965).

The creating of norms or expectations or rules is a natural part of group dynamics. Learners need a sense of structure and will feel psychologically safer if they know what is expected of them. They may already have come across institutional rules relating, for instance, to eating and drinking in ICT and other rooms, smoking, use of mobile phones, and specific subject-related Health and Safety regulations, as part of a more general induction programme. What we are now considering is more to do with attitudes and behaviours within the immediate teaching environment.

Activity 2.5

What do you think it would be useful to include in a set of ground rules for a group that you will teach?

Exactly what you have arrived at may well depend upon the nature and maturity of your learners and the setting within which you teach your particular subject.

Perhaps you may have considered:

- Punctuality, both at the beginning of sessions and returning from breaks
- Handing in work on time
- Avoidance of eating, drinking and mobile phones (if not already covered by institutional rules)

- Listening when attention is asked for
- Not talking whilst others are contributing
- Respecting rights of others to hold different points of view whether or not you agree with them
- Not being critical of or bullying others in the group
- Keeping all that is said within the group as confidential

Having established in your own mind what might be appropriate to include you need to decide how to agree these rules with your learners; some may be mandatory whilst others are negotiable. Essentially there are three positions that might be adopted here, as summarised in Figure 2.1.

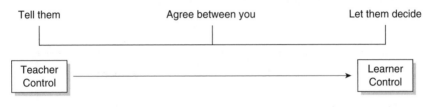

Figure 2.1

Which of the three positions is adopted is a matter of judgement and you may well use different strategies with different groups that you teach, but in arriving at a decision it is helpful to consider the following:

- The nature, size and maturity of the group may make one approach more appropriate than the others
- The confidence that you have in yourself and your ability to control or influence the group will affect the approach you choose to use
- The further towards the 'teacher control' end of the continuum you go, the more learners will consider the rules to be your rules and thus your responsibility to enforce them
- The further towards the 'learner control' end of the continuum you go, the more learners will see the rules as their rules and thus have a greater commitment to both the rules themselves and the enforcing of them

 Activity 2.6

I think the most appropriate method of setting ground rules for my groups is:

Ice-breakers

By this stage we will have established some rapport with our learners but we may also want learners to work and to learn together in a supportive manner. If this is the case, learners need to become acquainted and comfortable with each other.

This will take time but the process can be initiated by introducing an 'ice-breaker' at the start of teaching. An ice-breaker is any activity that encourages learners to talk to us, to each other and to the group as a whole. It is designed to break down the barriers that invariably exist when a group of people meets for the first time.

Ice-breakers range from 'short and sharp' to 'extended' activities and can be divided into the three categories shown in Figure 2.2.

Short and sharp

Extended

Category	Purpose
Introductions	To learn names and gain confidence by saying something in public
Activities	To learn names, encourage interaction and also promote learning related to the session objectives
Games	To learn names and also encourage interaction between group members

Figure 2.2

Some suggestions as to the form these might take are:

Introductions

- Learners introduce themselves and write their name on a card or label.
- Each learner interviews someone else and introduces them.
- Sitting in a circle, learners throw a ball to each other. Each time it is caught the learner gives their name and an interesting personal fact.

Activities

Activities need to focus on topics related to the subject and are best if these examine learners' previous experience.

- **Snowball**   Consider a chosen topic, for example the best way to study, individually, then in pairs, then in fours, then feed back to the whole group.
- **Alternate groups**   Learners introduce themselves in a group of four and discuss a given topic. Groups then re-form with learners joining a new group, introducing themselves and reporting the earlier discussion.
- **Expectations**   Learners form small groups, discuss their expectations of the course and report these on flipcharts on which they also write their names.

Games

- **Hello**   A piece of card is cut into four irregular pieces. Each learner is given a piece of card and has to form a group with learners having the three other fitting pieces. Each group then has to find a novel way of saying hello to the rest of the teaching group that includes stating their names.
- **Correct answers**   A question is asked (normally about an opinion) and three possible answers are offered. Learners form groups depending on what they think the answer is and then justify their choice to the rest of the teaching group.
- **Group logo**   Learners are randomly divided into small groups. Each small group devises a logo that includes information about group members.
- **Find a person who**   Learners are given a handout with boxes containing descriptions that might apply to another learner in the group. Examples could be: plays a sport, speaks a language in addition to English, plays a musical instrument, has a birthday in September. Each learner gains information from others until one person has names in all the boxes; then each learner introduces one other learner and one thing they now know about them. You can choose to devise descriptors which relate to your subject area.

There are many alternative ice-breakers to choose from and our choice is influenced by factors such as:

- The time available
- The subject matter
- How long the group will be together
- The size and nature of the group

Your particular teaching situation will determine which of the above are suitable as ice-breakers. The ice-breaker need not be a lengthy activity but invariably will help to encourage interaction and participation, thus getting the course off to a positive start.

Activity 2.7

Think about the next teaching you will deliver. Select an appropriate ice-breaker, either choosing from the list above or devising one of your own. Explain why you think it is an appropriate choice, making reference to the factors previously listed.

   I think the following ice-breaker would be suitable for my teaching situation:

   I think it is suitable because:

We have previously identified the sorts of actions by the teacher that have a negative effect on the climate of the course. The following list, although lengthy, is not exhaustive and you may wish to add to it, but it makes a start in identifying **good** practice. These are actions that will help the teacher promote a positive social and learning environment.

When we respond to learners, we:

- Are enthusiastic and show learners we are interested in them and their work
- Provide time and attention for each individual
- Treat learners in a consistent manner
- Involve learners in the teaching and encourage participation
- Give learners opportunities to demonstrate prowess

When we provide feedback, we:

- Focus on the positive, not on learners' mistakes
- Respond positively to all contributions
- Praise at every appropriate opportunity

When we communicate, we:

- Use positive body language (smiling, eye contact, approving gestures)
- Use language appropriate to learners
- Introduce technical terms with care, use jargon sparingly
- Make reference to areas we have in common with learners
- Use 'we' whenever possible ('We all agree that …')

It is important that we ensure learners feel comfortable in their learning and feel able to approach us with queries and problems. All of the above make a major contribution to lifting barriers so that very different learners all feel they can participate, contribute and make progress. As we will see in the next chapter, this is a key factor in motivation of learners.

Attention to the physical and social environments helps to put learners in the frame of mind that encourages them to participate fully in the process of communication, through which learning takes place. This process is essential to any teaching session and we next explore how effective communication can create a more successful learning environment.

Communication

Communication can be thought of as

the transfer of information from one person to another with the intention of bringing about a response.

There are many models of communication; their purpose is to help us understand the process more easily. The simplest is illustrated below:

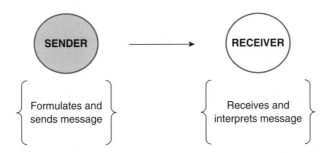

This could suggest that communication involves one person talking to another, who listens and takes in what is being said. This often happens in our teaching sessions when we are giving instructions or explanations. We use our voice to communicate. We all have different voices – some loud, some soft, some high, some low, some have distinct accents. Some of us like the sound of them; others do not. Whatever our voice, we can make the most of it by considering the following:

T → **Take your time**
A → **Alter the tone and pitch of your voice**
L → **Loud enough to be heard**
K → **Keep to an appropriate pace**

Take your time

Although we will be looking at pace of delivery later, it is worth remembering that whatever we say is more effective if we have thought it through, even if only briefly. Sometimes a slightly slower delivery or pause for thought can make a considerable difference as it allows us to 'engage brain before opening mouth'.

We all recognise the importance of the pause in everyday communication, but as teachers we do not always use it to best effect in teaching. Great communicators understand 'the art of the pause'. We may be feeling a little nervous and consequently not inclined to pause, as this may invite questions that we would prefer to avoid. If such feelings can be overcome, pauses can be used to good effect, provided they are not too long or used too frequently. Think back to teaching sessions in which you have been involved or even conversations you have had with friends. How were pauses used?

Activity 2.8

I have heard pauses being used to good effect in the following ways:

In completing the activity, you may have considered the following:

- Pausing before speaking or answering a question allows us to gather our thoughts and formulate a clearer response.
- Pausing allows the learner or group to prepare to receive our response.
- Pausing during instructing or explaining allows us to emphasise key points.
- Pausing allows our learners to absorb a number of consecutive points.
- Pausing after instructing, explaining or supplying the answer to a question signals that the point has now been dealt with and we are moving on to a new area.

Alter the tone and pitch of your voice

Sometimes a teacher's voice is described as boring or monotonous. This can lead to loss of attention or, in extreme cases, learners have been known to fall asleep! We can avoid this by varying the tone and pitch of our voices. When we are in conversation our voices become animated, rising and falling subconsciously, probably because conversations tend to be spontaneous. We plan and may rehearse our teaching, however, and this often leads to a more measured and flat delivery.

Sounds that are designed to capture attention (sirens on police cars and ambulances for instance) vary, altering their tone and pitch. We should try to remember this when teaching and use it to our advantage.

Loud enough to be heard

We do not have difficulty in judging how loud our voice should be when talking with a friend. We automatically adjust to our surroundings, whether we are in a quiet or a noisy room, next to each other or some distance apart. As the number of people we are talking to increases this becomes more difficult. This is why it can be hard for us to judge the appropriate volume level for our voice when teaching.

Sometimes we need help with this and it is not uncommon for teachers to ask if they can be heard at the back of the room. The volume we are looking for is reached when everyone can hear but it is not uncomfortably loud. Rather than ask our learners if they can hear, we can achieve an appropriate volume in a teaching environment by focusing on the learners at the back of the room and talking to them. This has the effect of achieving a volume that suits all the learners in the room. Sometimes, however, we may choose to use a quieter voice to good effect in order to give emphasis to the point we are making.

Keep to an appropriate pace

In deciding on an appropriate pace we will need to bear a number of factors in mind. In the next Activity box you are asked to identify factors you think have an influence on your pace of delivery.

Activity 2.9

I think my pace of delivery is affected by:

Our normal speaking rate is about 140 words per minute and this is manageable for most listeners. If we talk faster than this, learners will find it hard work to process the information. If, on the other hand, we talk more slowly we may well lose their attention.

The previous knowledge and experience of our learners will have a bearing on the rate at which they can receive and process information. If we are communicating new and fairly complex information, learners will need more time to process and file it away (even with appropriate use of pauses) and so a slower pace is required. If we are communicating information with which they have some familiarity, or the information is simple or less important, merely providing background or repetition, our pace of delivery can be quicker.

Pace of delivery is also affected by other factors, such as the number of learners we are addressing. How confident we feel about our material and the time available to us will also have an effect on the pacing of delivery. An awareness of all these factors will help us determine the most appropriate pace of delivery. To check this, we need to note the response that learners are making and this is where 'non-verbal' cues play an important part. We shall be looking at these in the following pages.

So, we communicate with learners by talking to them. Similarly, they talk to us. Therefore both listening and talking are important skills in the communication process. Our model of communication has now become a little more complex.

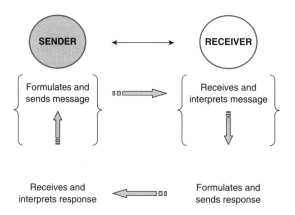

We are now considering communication to be a two-way process involving listening as well as talking. Listening involves:

- Clearing the mind ready to receive the message
- Focusing on what is being said rather than thinking about our reply
- Checking that our interpretation is correct

To make communication productive, both parties need to recognise that each is participating fully. It is easy to know when someone is talking as we can hear the words, but how do we know when someone is listening? We need to regard listening as an **active** process, in which signals are sent to the other person to let them know we are listening.

Active listening is recognised by a range of non-verbal cues, such as:

- Eye contact
- Nodding
- Leaning forward
- Alert facial expressions
- Open body language

Verbally, we show active listening largely through a technique known as summarising. This involves phrases such as:

Active listening, then, shows the learner that we are interested in what they have to say. This helps to promote the climate of openness and trust that is important to establish effective communication.

Non-verbal communication

So far we have largely explored communication that uses the spoken word, but it can be argued that although we speak with our voice, we communicate with our whole body, as has been seen in active listening.

Simple things like whether we stand or sit to address our learners, our posture and the expression on our face, all send messages that play as important a role in the communication process as the words we use. Such **non-verbal** signals have a significant effect on the way in which our learners receive and interpret messages. These must now be added to our model of the communication process:

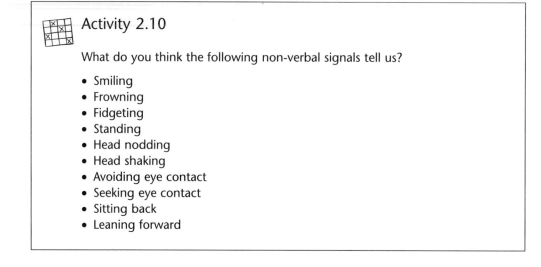

Activity 2.10

What do you think the following non-verbal signals tell us?

- Smiling
- Frowning
- Fidgeting
- Standing
- Head nodding
- Head shaking
- Avoiding eye contact
- Seeking eye contact
- Sitting back
- Leaning forward

Interpreting non-verbal communication can be difficult, particularly as different cues can have a variety of interpretations depending on the cultural context, but it does add another important dimension to our understanding of the communication process.

From the learner's perspective, our smiles, posture, demeanour and appearance contribute much to our acceptance, rapport and initial credibility. All of these can therefore influence how our message is received.

We often use our hands to help interpretation and to give emphasis, but perhaps the most important aspect of non-verbal communication is eye contact. In normal conversation we would expect to maintain a considerable degree of eye contact. Indeed, avoiding eye contact would give the conversation an uncomfortable or awkward feel. When we talk to a group of people, however, eye contact with each individual is far less frequent, but remains just as significant and important to the success of the communication process.

A lack of eye contact when we teach can be interpreted as a lack of confidence on our part. It can lead to learners not feeling part of what is going on; attention and involvement can subsequently decrease. It is important therefore, when we are engaged in teaching, that we make a conscious effort to make eye contact with everyone in the group. This will have the effect of making everyone feel part of the communication process; it helps us to judge understanding and decide on the pacing of activities.

Barriers to communication

So far we have considered the positive aspects of non-verbal communication, but sometimes it can provide a distraction and take attention away from the information being communicated. If we are nervous, for instance, our arms and hands seem to become larger and more obvious. What do we do with them when we are not using them to help interpretation or provide emphasis? We could, perhaps, run our fingers through our hair, straighten our clothes, play with watches, rings, or loose change, or stroke our necks or foreheads. All of these provide distractions that hinder the communication process. Anything that interferes with getting the message across is termed a **barrier to communication**, which we should seek to avoid.

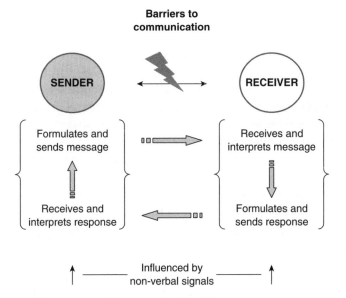

Distractions by the non-verbal communications of the teacher are just one type of barrier.

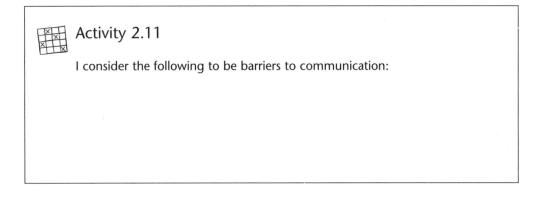

Activity 2.11

I consider the following to be barriers to communication:

The barriers you have identified will depend on your previous experience; for example, someone who is hearing-impaired and needs to lip read may find a moustache that masks lip movement a major barrier to communication. Whatever your previous experience, the barriers will probably fall into one of two categories:

External barriers

Physical – noise, interruptions, discomfort (hot, airless, cold, too light or dark, poor acoustics)
Language – strong accent or dialect, technical language, other jargon
Relevance – too theoretical, no relationship to learners' experience or role
Lack of rapport – with teacher, other learners

It is within our power as teachers to deal with the problems caused by many of the external barriers. We can alter seating arrangements to accommodate more participation. We can minimise the effects of noise and interruptions. We can try to adjust heat and light to appropriate levels. We can introduce relevant practical examples whenever possible rather than being too theoretical or using excessive technical terms or jargon.

We can also take care with language, ensuring that neither we nor our learners give offence. Language or terms that contain negative overtones relating to race, gender, culture, sexual orientation, age or disability should be avoided and more positive words and phrases used.

We can establish rapport using ice-breakers. Sometimes, however, the barriers are difficult for us to identify as, rather than being caused by the teaching environment, they may be internal barriers, personal to learners.

Internal barriers

Psychological – preoccupation with other matters, lack of interest, or confidence
Past experience – preconceptions, dislike of learning methods, stereotyping
Resistance to change – dislike of something new
Personal – mistrust of teacher, teacher's motives, prejudice

Internal barriers are much more difficult to deal with than external barriers. We may not even be aware of them, although their effects may well be apparent. The first step in dealing with internal barriers is to identify them. This is unlikely to happen unless we have created an appropriate social and learning environment, as described earlier in this chapter. The most common internal barriers we encounter as teachers are related to learner motivation and we shall look at this in the next chapter.

Chapter summary

The main points covered in this chapter are:

✓ The learning environment has a physical, social and learning component, each of which has to be managed by the teacher
✓ Communication can be a one-way, two-way or several-way process
✓ The way in which the physical and social environments are managed impact upon patterns of communication
✓ First impressions are important in establishing a positive learning environment

- ✓ Ground rules contribute to effective learning and the setting of these can be led by either teachers or learners
- ✓ There are a number of ways of 'breaking the ice' and helping groups to gel
- ✓ Effective use of voice depends upon a number of factors
- ✓ Active listening is an important aspect of the communication process
- ✓ Communication can be non-verbal as well as verbal
- ✓ Barriers to communication can be both external and internal

Solution to Activity 2.2 on p. 18.

We think you will agree with this summary: Arrangement 1 = two-way; Arrangement 2 = one-way; Arrangement 3 = several-ways.

→ References

Tuckman, B (1965) Developmental sequence in small groups. *Psychological Bulletin*, 63, 384–99. The article was reprinted in *Group Facilitation: A Research and Applications Journal*, Number 3, Spring 2001, and is available as a Word document at: http://dennislearningcenter.osu.edu/references/GROUP%20DEV%20ARTICLE.doc

Further reading

Jaques, D. and Salmon, G. (2007) *Learning in Groups: A Handbook for Face-to-Face and Online Environments*, (4th Edn) London: Routledge.
See Chapter 4 of this book for a very readable discussion of communication, barriers to communication and giving feedback.

Siddons, S. (2008) *The Complete Presentation Skills Handbook.* London: Kogan Page.
Although this is not a book specifically about teaching, you may want to look at Chapter 10, 'Voice and Performance Skills', and Chapter 11, 'Nerves and Body Language'.

Useful websites

Non-verbal communication

   http://nonverbal.ucsc.edu/

   http://lynn_meade.tripod.com/id56.htm

Ice-breakers

   www.icebreakers.ws

Active listening

   http://toolboxes.flexiblelearning.net.au/demosites/series2/205/SEGMENTS/INTCLNTS/Actvlist.htm

Voice projection

   www.triadpublishing.com/speakers.shtml

Motivating learners and managing behaviour

> **Chapter overview**
>
> **When you have worked through this chapter on motivation and managing behaviour you will be able to:**
>
> - **Distinguish between intrinsic and extrinsic motivation**
> - **List strategies that may be used to increase learner motivation**
> - **Describe approaches to behaviour management which use rewards and sanctions**
> - **Identify the role of self-concept in causing inappropriate behaviour**
> - **Describe ways of changing self-concept from a negative to a positive perspective**
> - **Differentiate between aggressive, passive and assertive responses to inappropriate behaviour**

Each time we meet a new group of lifelong learners, the only certainty that we can rely on is that they will all have their own particular needs, characteristics and peculiarities. They will all be individuals in their own right. It is coping with this range of different personalities and aptitudes, and helping individuals learn and form as a group, that makes teaching in the lifelong learning sector both challenging and rewarding.

Motivation

Although the learners themselves are different, they all go through a similar process in their learning. This allows general principles to be identified that can guide us in making learning more effective. Generally, learning is more effective when:

1   We are motivated to want to learn
2   We can focus and hold attention on the material we are learning
3   We readily understand the material
4   The material is presented in a format that matches our natural learning style
5   We can hold the material in our memory
6   We can use what we have learned in real life situations
7   We feel valued and acknowledged by others in the learning environment

Of the areas outlined above, **motivation** is a key issue as, without it, it is unlikely that learners will progress. There are lots of different theories of motivation which seem to fall into one of two opposing perspectives.

One view of motivation considers it to be a process that is controlled by factors in our immediate environment. These factors are external to us as a person and so the term used to express this viewpoint is **extrinsic motivation**.

The opposing view regards our own internal needs to be the controlling factor as these are what drive or motivate us to do what we do. This type of motivation is termed **intrinsic motivation**.

 ## Activity 3.1

In the table below, indicate with an 'I' or an 'E' whether you consider the example illustrates intrinsic (I) or extrinsic (E) motivation

Example	I/E?
To gain a qualification	
The learner finds the material interesting	
To receive a pay rise	
To gain the approval of others	
To satisfy curiosity	
The teacher is enthusiastic	
To meet people	
To discover if 'I can'	
To gain promotion	
To increase self-confidence	
To receive praise	
To learn something new	
To learn for the fun of it	

Extrinsic factors include qualifications, a pay rise, the approval of others, meeting other people, promotion, praise and, last but by no means least, the model of enthusiasm provided by the teacher, regardless of the particular subject to be covered, group to be taught or time of day.

Extrinsic motivation is an area on which we as teachers can have an effect. Extrinsic motivators, after all, come from the environment and as teachers we are managers of the learning environment. Some extrinsic motivators, such as pay rises and promotion, are not within our control, but there are plenty of other options open to us.

Some relate to the teacher and their actions

- Present an enthusiastic role model
- Be professional but approachable
- Make learners feel they matter
- Use praise freely but only when deserved
- Give constructive, positive feedback

Others are concerned with the environment

- Provide appropriate facilities and conditions
- Create a supportive environment where everyone feels part of the group
- Set a relaxed but purposeful atmosphere in which mistakes are not ridiculed
- Communicate using a range of media that suit each learner's needs

Others relate to the way in which teaching sessions are conducted

- Give learners the opportunity to participate in setting their own goals
- Set tasks that are challenging but achievable
- Encourage active participation in the session

A much-quoted model of motivation is that of Maslow (1943), which is summarised in Figure 3.1 in relation to the teaching and learning context. Maslow considers motivation to be intrinsic. Individuals are driven by inner needs, some of which are identified in the list. Maslow maintains that some of these needs take priority over others – they exist in a hierarchy.

The order of satisfying these needs starts at the bottom of the list and works its way up to the top, so needs of the body (physiological) take precedence over all of the others and achieving individual potential (self-actualisation) is only addressed when all of the needs below it in the list have been satisfied.

Looking back at the previous chapter on setting an appropriate environment, it can be seen that Physiological and Safety needs are part of the physical environment, Belonging and Esteem needs fall within the social environment and Self-actualisation is what is strived for in the learning environment. Maslow confirms then that there is a need to address the physical and social environments before motivation is focused on learning. More importantly for our present discussion, Maslow suggests that what motivates learners is the need to achieve their potential.

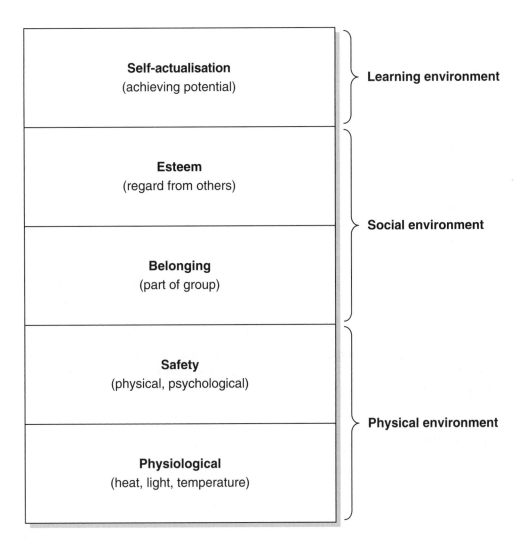

Figure 3.1 Summary of Maslow's model of motivation

Generally, intrinsic motivators such as the need to self-actualise are more powerful motivators than extrinsic motivators. Intrinsic motivators are also more effective in bringing about learning as they focus on the actual learning itself rather than what results from it or the context in which it is set.

Some of our learners are intrinsically motivated when we first meet them and have a clear aim to achieve their individual potential; the task then is to maintain their motivation at that level. Others, however, may not be motivated in this way and so the task here is not to maintain but to foster intrinsic motivation.

If doctors wish to treat an ailment they must first of all know what is causing it, to arrive at the most appropriate treatment strategy. The same applies to motivation. If we wish to bring about motivation in learners, we can decide how to go about this if we have some idea of the reasons for its initial absence.

Activity 3.2

List the reasons why learners may be demotivated

1

2

3

4

5

Your list is probably quite lengthy as there are many potential reasons for learners being demotivated. Perhaps motivation has been blunted by lack of success in previous experiences of learning or it may be that attendance is not voluntary.

Now think about the reasons you have listed above. In the next activity, pick out three of these and then identify strategies you could use to improve the situation in each case. You may find it useful to refer back to the list of extrinsic motivators to help you in this task.

Activity 3.3

Strategies for improving motivation

	Reason	Strategy I would employ
1		
2		
3		

We can affect motivation, then, by working on extrinsic factors with the intention that, as time progresses, these will bring about a shift towards intrinsic motivation. If learners come on your course to achieve qualifications, for instance, you can boost their motivation by being enthusiastic yourself; giving your approval through praise and by showing them they are succeeding. Your learners will, with any luck, gradually become more interested in the content and enjoy learning and so motivation is progressively internalised.

Approaches to behaviour management

Teachers consider the management of motivation to be an important skill, since high levels of motivation are key to effective learning. Conversely, low levels of motivation make learning less likely but, more seriously, can lead to difficult or challenging behaviours on the part of some learners.

 Activity 3.4

What behaviours might you consider as difficult or challenging?

It is unlikely that you will have noted many, if any, examples of serious confrontation between learners and teachers or open challenges to the teacher's authority. Your examples are more likely to fall into the category of what two reports on school discipline (Elton Report, 1989; Steer Report, 2005) call 'low level disruption'.

Low level disruption can be thought of as any form of behaviour that prevents teachers teaching or learners learning and typically includes:

- Persistently talking to each other
- Distracting others from their work
- Making unnecessary (non-verbal) noise
- Fooling around (throwing paper aeroplanes etc.)
- Asking inappropriate questions
- Using mobile phones and texting
- Reading magazines or newspapers
- 'Winding up' the teacher
- Withdrawing completely from the session

Whilst none of these might be considered as extremely serious in themselves, they disturb the flow of the session. This can interfere with learning and the cumulative effects are draining for teachers. Perhaps more importantly, over a period of time such behaviours, if not addressed, can create a climate in which the likelihood of more serious incidents is increased.

We have seen the diverse nature of lifelong learning and learners in Chapter 1 and the vast majority of our learners are unlikely to pose such problems. The remainder of this chapter, therefore, needs to be read and interpreted within the perspective of your own particular working context and adapted as necessary.

There are two general views of inappropriate behaviour:

- The behaviours themselves are the problem and must be dealt with directly
- The behaviours are ways of highlighting an underlying problem and it is the cause of this problem that must be identified and dealt with, leading to the disappearance of the symptoms

Neither view will generate successful strategies if we do not consider ourselves as role models in interactions, jointly contributing to solutions we would like to see.

If you subscribe to the first view of inappropriate behaviour your strategies will revolve around rules, rewards and sanctions. We have already referred to ground rules and the different ways of arriving at these in Chapter 2. Ground rules are a method of regulating behaviour.

A similar method is that employed by 'assertive discipline' approaches in which learners are encouraged to choose to behave in an appropriate manner through a system of rewards and consequences. Assertive discipline consists of three parts:

1 A number of rules (usually about five – the fewer rules the more effective the approach) that are to be followed at all times by all learners, who are fully aware of what they are.
2 A system of awarding positive recognition to all learners following the rules.
3 A series of consequences that follow a choice not to follow the rules. The level of consequence is proportional to the severity or frequency of rule breaking and again all learners are fully aware of these consequences.

You can find out more about this approach by following up the suggested reading and web links at the end of the chapter.

To understand the second view of inappropriate behaviour we need to identify the reasons behind the behaviours that concern us.

Activity 3.5

Why do you think learners exhibit the behaviours you identified in the previous exercise?

The causes of challenging behaviour can range from boredom to testing the teacher's resolve and ability to maintain order; from diverting attention from feelings of inadequacy to 'having a laugh'; from conforming to group norms to maintaining a sense of individuality.

Self-concept

Of particular interest is the notion of diverting attention from feelings of inadequacy. Psychology tells us that we all have a particular way of thinking of ourselves – our self-concept. This consists of two parts: self-image, which is the more fact-based 'self-portrait' we have of ourselves; and self-esteem, which is concerned with the worth or value that we place upon ourselves. Our self-concepts are shaped by our previous experience and the responses and feedback we experience 'in the moment'. These influence and shape the way we behave. To some extent, self-concept is also dependent on the context within which we find ourselves. You might be the life and soul of the party talking to friends in an informal setting, for instance, but be terrified of giving a talk to a group of strangers.

The self-concept we exhibit in a learning environment is often known as the 'academic' self-concept. Suppose you have a positive academic self-concept; your previous experiences of learning are of success and you therefore expect a similar outcome in your current learning. You know that if you try hard and show a positive attitude towards your work you are likely to reap the rewards of your efforts. Your energy will thus be channelled into your work rather than inappropriate behaviour.

If, on the other hand, you have a negative academic self-concept, the picture is rather different. In a learning situation you will expect to experience difficulty or perhaps ultimately fail altogether. You will feel anxious and unsure of yourself. Your main aim will be to avoid further failure and, for you, applying yourself to the work in hand does not achieve this. You do have a number of other strategies you can resort to, however. You can blame your teacher for your failure; you can withdraw from the lesson or engage in a number of avoidance techniques such as not bringing pens, pencils or any necessary equipment to the session. If pushed to work you can simply refuse, as the consequences of refusal are preferable to the consequences of failure. All of these strategies can be perceived as or lead to challenging behaviour.

Developing a positive self-concept

Lifelong learning is often referred to as 'the second chance' and so a proportion of learners we encounter may well have a background of previous lack of educational success. If we subscribe to the second view of inappropriate behaviour, our efforts will be less concerned with behaviour itself, focusing more on bringing about a positive academic self-concept, thus removing the need for the learner to behave in a challenging manner.

Activity 3.6

How could you bring about a positive change in academic self-concept?

As one of the key causes of negative self-concept in a learner is lack of success, your responses to the above exercise will no doubt be largely concerned with achieving success in learning and recognising such successes. This may be achieved through:

- Setting regular short-term goals
- Agreeing individual targets which are challenging but achievable
- Making learning active
- Ensuring learners know exactly what is to be achieved and why
- Breaking tasks down into shorter, manageable 'chunks'
- Starting with simpler, straightforward tasks and gradually increasing the complexity
- Creating time for more one-to-one contact
- Looking for the positives in learners' work
- Showing that you expect them to be successful
- Encouraging learners to reflect and build upon their successes
- Recording and pointing out progress
- Using praise to acknowledge success

and, most important of all

- Listening to what learners have to say

Responses to inappropriate behaviour

These two views of behaviour provide different ways of approaching the problems posed by challenging behaviour in the teaching situation. There will be occasions when we need to tackle behaviour directly; for example when it constitutes a health and safety risk. There will be other times when we will be looking for a longer-term solution by tackling the root cause of the behaviour. Effective behaviour management invariably involves a combination of each approach in appropriate measures.

Some groups will contain higher proportions than others of learners exhibiting challenging behaviour. Interestingly, however, not all individuals or groups demonstrate the same degree of inappropriate behaviour with all of their teachers. Some 14–16 year olds in a college environment revealed the following thoughts about who were considered to be 'good' teachers, for whom they behaved well.

Clearly, the relationship between teacher and learners is important but reaching an understanding of what is being taught and a sense of having achieved something also play their part. Although these views are expressed by 14–16 year-olds, they could equally well apply to your learners or to any learner within the sector.

Normally, learners will not present difficult behaviour if they feel that they are valued and are getting something from the session, so teachers who themselves behave appropriately and who create a positive learning environment (refer back to Chapter 2) are less likely to encounter difficult behaviour from their learners.

Various studies have come to the conclusion that good classroom management, accompanied by good inter-personal skills, is key in pre-empting difficult behaviour – 'nipping it in the bud' before it becomes serious.

Effective practice in this area can include the following:

Beginning sessions

- Be in the room first, greet learners individually, if possible, making good eye contact
- Attitude is important – if you show that you are pleased to be there, perhaps they will be as well!
- Have a 'starter' activity ready, giving an active and purposeful beginning
- Show you are well prepared and confident
- Explain simply but clearly what is to be achieved in the session and why it will be useful

During sessions

- Make sure learners are occupied throughout the session in relevant and sufficiently challenging activities
- Make sure that activities are clearly explained and have a purpose
- Expect a definite 'end product' to an activity and make sure learners are aware of time limits, without creating too much pressure
- Use a differentiated approach so all are engaged in stretching but achievable work
- Maintain the momentum of the session – try to avoid periods of inactivity, no matter how short
- Think where best to position yourself in the room at different stages of the session; the more confidently you move around the room and interact with learners, the less confrontational the situation is likely to be
- Show you are aware of potential problems and deal with them quickly before they can escalate

Ending sessions

- Leave sufficient time for an ordered ending to the session
- Acknowledge the learning that has taken place
- Identify progress and give praise if appropriate

Smith and Laslett (1993) have devised 'four rules of classroom management' and in these suggest that, of the above stages, it is the management of the beginnings and endings of sessions that is crucial in maintaining good order.

Sometimes, however, more serious instances of challenging behaviour can occur and need to be handled appropriately to defuse matters and prevent an escalation of the situation. Sometimes it is not so much what we do that is the biggest influence in these situations, but rather how we do it. It is not what we say to the learner who is being difficult, but the manner in which we say it that matters the most. Emotions can run high on both sides in any form of confrontation and play their part in affecting the outcome. Consider the following activity:

Activity 3.7

What feelings might be aroused in teachers when confronted with a challenge to their authority?

Whenever we are faced by a situation we perceive as threatening, adrenalin is released into the body, readying it to respond to the perceived threat by fighting or running away. This is known as fight-or-flight response. A fight response is accompanied by feelings of anger, flight by feelings of apprehension. It is this emotional reaction that determines how we subsequently act.

If a teacher feels angry when faced with a perceived challenge to their authority, their reaction is likely to be aggressive. The language used would be characterised by:

- Criticism – 'can't you get it right even after I've explained it to you twice?'
- Sarcasm – 'even my grandmother knows that'
- Blunt refusals – 'of course you can't do that'
- Strong commands – 'I won't tell you again, just stop that now!'
- Grudging praise – 'well I suppose it's better than your last effort'

and would be accompanied by aggressive body language and tone of voice.

Activity 3.8

If you are addressed in an aggressive manner, how does it make you feel and how are you likely to react?

Acting aggressively will invariably provoke a similarly aggressive response from the learner and soon the situation becomes more confrontational and can spiral out of control.

If, on the other hand, apprehension is the primary emotion aroused, the teacher will offer a much more passive reaction. The type of language used in this instance would be characterised by:

- An inability to say 'no' – 'perhaps it's best if you don't do that just now'
- Avoidance of direct instruction – 'now it might be a good idea if you waited till after break'
- Avoidance of direct criticism – 'personally I think it's quite good but I don't think the examiner would agree'
- Allocating blame – 'I know it's quite soon to hand in work but the Course Leader set that date'

and again accompanied by corresponding tone of voice and body language.

Activity 3.9

If you are addressed in a passive manner, how does it make you feel and how would you react?

A passive reaction from the teacher can leave learners confused, lacking in direction and ultimately more frustrated than they were to start with. They can feel that the teacher is not sufficiently concerned to make a commitment.

Quite often then, if we act from the emotion of the moment, the ways in which we handle difficult situations can be counterproductive. Watkins (1997) suggests a sequence of:

1 **Feel**   Initial emotive reaction
2 **Think**   Refer back to previous experience and knowledge
3 **Do**   Now decide on and carry through a course of action

The examples above illustrate **Feel** and **Do**, missing out the second stage of **Think**; Watkins refers to this combination as **reacting**. He suggests that it is far more productive to complete the whole sequence, thus **responding** rather than reacting. If we respond, we are basing our actions around a rational rather than emotional backdrop. Our state of mind is calm rather than angry or apprehensive and so our response is assertive.

It is important that we learn to be emotionally self-aware and manage our own behaviours and relationships appropriately. All social interactions are a shared responsibility and we need to recognise our own role in generating learner reactions.

The type of language used in an assertive response can be characterised by:

- Clear instructions with reasons – 'I want you to sit down now as you are distracting others from their work'
- Says no but with reasons – 'you can't do it that way as it might catch fire'
- Encourages learners to express themselves – 'you say you disagree but what exactly are your reasons for this?'
- Includes praise when offering criticism – 'although you haven't produced much work, you started off really well'

once more accompanied by corresponding tone of voice and body language.

Activity 3.10

If you were addressed in an assertive manner, how would it make you feel and what would your likely reaction be?

Assertive responses can defuse difficult situations.

There are a number of techniques associated with assertiveness, and a summary of these can be found on the website listed at the end of the chapter.

In this chapter we have looked at some aspects of dealing with inappropriate behaviours. Our review aims to give you some ideas against which to examine your own practice and suggests further avenues to explore.

As a final thought, here are some reflections on their own practice by a group of teachers who teach 'disaffected' learners. Perhaps they contain good advice regardless of who our learners are?

- We try not to be confrontational
- We encourage learners to take responsibility for their own behaviour
- We have ground rules – ideally set by learners
- We always act promptly at the first sign of trouble
- We sometimes get down to their level
- We nag (because I want you to succeed)
- We give occasional incentives
- We give learners choices whenever we can
- We listen to learners and generally aim to be approachable

Chapter summary

The main points covered in this chapter are:

✓ Motivation can be internal to learners (intrinsic) or come from an outside source (extrinsic)
✓ Maslow's Hierarchy of Needs is a model of intrinsic motivation
✓ As teachers, we use methods of extrinsic motivation to promote intrinsic motivation in learners
✓ Inappropriate behaviour can be managed by strategies such as setting ground rules and 'assertive discipline'
✓ A poor 'academic self-concept' can lead to difficult or challenging behaviour. Strategies aimed at improving self-concept result in improved behaviour
✓ Effective classroom management can prevent inappropriate behaviour
✓ Aggressive or passive reactions to challenging behaviour can lead to escalation. Assertive responses can defuse difficult situations

→ References

The Elton Report (1989) *Discipline in Schools: Report of the Committee of Enquiry chaired by Lord Elton.* London: HMSO.

Maslow, A.H. (1943) A Theory of Human Motivation, *Psychological Review* 50 (1943): 370–96.

Smith, C. and Laslett, R. (1993) *Effective Classroom Management: A Teacher's Guide.* London: Routledge

The Steer Report (2005) *Learning Behaviour: The Report of The Practitioners' Group on School Behaviour and Discipline, chaired by Sir Alan Steer.* London: DfES

Watkins, C. (1997) *Managing Classroom Behaviour.* London: Association of Teachers and Lecturers.

📖 Further reading

Vizard, D. (2007) *How to Manage Behaviour in Further Education.* London: Paul Chapman Publishing.
A user-friendly approach which looks specifically at Further Education and 14–16 in particular. Practical rather than theoretical, covering all aspects of difficult behaviour, comes complete with a CD of Staff Development exercises.

Wallace, S. (2007) *Managing Behaviour in the Lifelong Learning Sector,* (2nd Edn). Exeter: Learning Matters.
Written for the lifelong learning sector, this looks at motivation and behaviour in a common-sense manner. Contains lots of case studies for analysis and reflection.

🖱 Useful websites

Assertive discipline

http://maxweber.hunter.cuny.edu/pub/eres/EDSPC715_MCINTYRE/AssertiveDiscipline.html

www.derby.ac.uk/telmie/private/plymouth/socemassdisc.htm

www.teamtechnology.co.uk/assertiveness/how-to-be-more-assertive-part12.html

Starting to plan

Chapter overview

When you have worked through this chapter on planning you will be able to:

- Identify the reasons for planning teaching
- List the factors to be taken into consideration when planning sessions
- Identify the sequence of planning decisions involved in the teaching cycle
- Define and distinguish between aims and learning objectives
- Write clear aims and learning objectives for sessions
- Identify factors influencing your choice of method
- Identify a range of learning methods and select appropriate methods

All the chapters in this book start with a box outlining what you will be able to do upon completion. Look back at the box at the top of this page and read its contents again. You now have a clear idea of what you will be covering in this chapter, so the information contained in the box is very helpful to you. The contents of the box are commonly called the 'learning objectives' or 'learning outcomes' for this chapter. The two terms can be defined differently but are often used interchangeably, so for the sake of simplicity we will stick to the term 'learning objective'.

We found it helpful, in writing this book, to decide on the intended 'learning objectives' prior to developing each chapter. Before we could consider what should be included in this chapter on planning for teaching, **we** needed to decide what **you** should be able to do in order to be successful in planning and preparing your teaching sessions. Until we had made this decision, we could not start to think about appropriate content, activities and checks on learning. You will also find this systematic approach useful in your own planning.

This chapter focuses on the process of planning in general and specifically on the decisions you will make prior to delivering any form of teaching. These decisions are recorded on a written plan (see Chapter 12 for detail and formats). When you have worked through this chapter, you should be able to develop plans for your own sessions that will make clear:

- What you are trying to achieve – the learning objective(s)

In future chapters we will look at:

- What methods you will select
- What resources you will choose
- How you will assess and then review what you have done

Why plan?

Before we begin to examine the decisions on which we base our planning, we must first appreciate **why** we plan. As you will realise, professionals in the lifelong learning sector lead busy lives with little enough time to fulfil all of the roles and responsibilities discussed in Chapter 1. Why spend precious time devising plans for teaching sessions? What are the advantages?

If we plan and prepare something first, then whatever we do will be more effective and, in the long term, will save us time. If we write out a list before we go shopping, for instance, we are more likely to come back with all the things we need. Similarly, if you write a session plan you are more likely to conduct your teaching in an organised and systematic manner.

What to consider in planning

In the same way that a shopping list is a record of decisions we make before we go shopping, a session plan is a record of all the decisions we will have to make before teaching. Deciding what to include on a shopping list is quite easy. We decide what meals to make, we look around our kitchen shelves to see which ingredients we already have, note which items we are missing and then we write our list. What to include in a session plan is not as straightforward. There are many more factors to think about and decide upon.

What do you think you will have to consider before you run a teaching session? List your thoughts in the activity box below:

 Activity 4.1

List all the things you might consider in order to plan effectively for a session:

Perhaps you included some or all of the following:

- Length of the session
- Time of day
- Room/venue
- Individual learners' prior knowledge and experience
- Individual support needs
- Size and mix of group
- Learning objectives
- Content
- Teaching notes
- Visual aids
- Other resources or materials
- Teaching methods
- Activities for learners
- External requirements
- How to check learning has occurred

This is quite an extensive list. Which item do we consider first? Is there a logical order? How do we record everything on a plan?

The sequence in planning

In the last activity, when you listed factors to consider prior to teaching, did you think of the things you listed in any particular order or did they just tumble onto the page? Is there a set order in which to think about these or might the order be different each time you plan? We hope you will agree that there is a particular order in which to plan a teaching session.

Consider the following: when you are going on holiday you will find there are a lot of decisions to be made. We have listed some of them below:

- Which clothes will you take?
- How will you get there?
- Where will you go?
- How much money will you need?
- Where will you stay?

Activity 4.2

Put the holiday decisions above into a logical order:

You will probably agree with the order below:

1   Where to go
2   Where to stay
3   How to get there
4   What money to take
5   Which clothes to take

We have chosen this order because until you have decided where you want to go, you cannot make an informed decision about the remaining travel arrangements. You will feel rather silly, for instance, if you decide first on clothes to take (swimsuit, sunglasses), how to get there (by train) and then decide to go to Alaska. If going to Alaska is your starting point, then it is easy to come to a decision as to how to get there; you want to get there quickly and so you will fly. You can now decide what money and which clothes to take.

As you can see, there is a logical sequence in making these decisions: 1 and 2 above refer to your destination, 3 refers to method of travel, and 4 and 5 identify what you will need to take. A similar logic applies to the decisions you make before teaching.

Holiday decisions	Teaching decisions
1 Where will I go?	1 What is to be learned?
2 How will I get there?	2 What methods are to be used?
3 What will I take?	3 What resources are appropriate?

Under normal circumstances, however, if you go on holiday to somewhere you have not visited before, you need to know if you have arrived at the right destination. You will want to check, 'Am I at the Hotel Iceberg in Alaska?' and make sure you are in the right place.

Later on, back home, you may think about returning for a future holiday. This decision would be based on looking back over your recent experience and seeing if you thought everything went well. Did you like the scenery? Was it easy to get to? How was the accommodation? Next time you might decide to go somewhere else rather than Alaska, or go to Alaska but stay in another hotel, based upon your experiences of this year.

When we conduct any form of teaching we also need to know if we have reached our destination. Have our learners achieved what we wanted them to? We would also think about whether we would teach in this way again. We might change the session totally next time or adjust it. We now have two further stages to add to our sequence:

Holiday decisions	Teaching decisions
1 Where will I go?	1 What is to be learned?
2 How will I get there?	2 What methods are to be used?
3 What will I take?	3 What resources are appropriate?
4 How will I check I have reached the correct destination?	4 How is learning to be checked?
5 Was this a good holiday? Would I do it again?	5 What changes (if any) would I make to this session if I were to do it again?

We now have a sequence of decisions to make before we engage in the planning of any teaching. Before we can start to make these decisions, however, we need to consider the needs that have to be met by the teaching we plan. We will want to ask questions about the needs of:

• The syllabus/curriculum/award body requirements
• The teacher (ourselves)
• The learners

Considering these will help us decide the form and content of the teaching, but in terms of the actual delivery, the learners and their needs are our first consideration.

Activity 4.3

Why should we consider learners first when planning delivery of a session?

You will have identified a number of reasons why learners might be our first consideration; perhaps the proof of this is in the fact that no two teaching sessions are the same. Although the same learning may be involved, we modify each session to respond to the particular group we are teaching. This is because the learners are different each time and we need to take these differences into account. Differences in learners may relate to characteristics such as motivation, previous experience, personality, gender, age and other factors that we will consider in a later chapter.

If we consider learner characteristics beforehand, we can make decisions tailored to the needs of specific groups and focus our teaching more effectively. Sometimes you will not meet your learners until the time of teaching, but the more you can find out about them in advance, the more informed your planning decisions will be.

We have now identified all of the considerations we need to take into account in our teaching; the full sequence of planning decisions is summarised below:

Decisions	What we do
Who are our learners?	Analyse learners' **needs**
What is it we are trying to teach?	Write teaching **aims**
What is to be learned?	Write **learning objectives**
How is learning to take place?	Decide on **methods**/learning activities
What is needed to assist learning?	Identify **resources**
How will the learning be identified?	Decide on how to **assess** learning
How would this session be modified in the future?	Select methods to **evaluate** the session

You will notice that some specific teaching terms appear in the second column. These will be dealt with in more detail as you progress through the book. If you would like a brief definition of these terms at this stage, please refer to the glossary at the back of the book.

The decisions above have been presented as a list, but you will notice that the outcome of the last decision will inform the whole planning process next time around. It is therefore useful to view the planning process as a cycle with each particular stage informing the next (Figure 4.1).

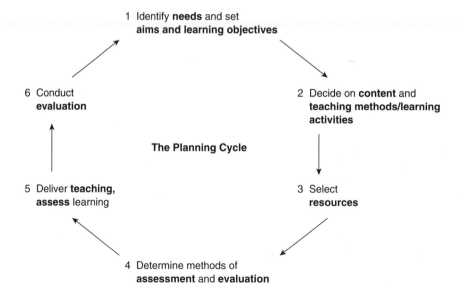

Figure 4.1

Aims and objectives

After considering the needs of learners, planning starts with aims; but what is meant by the term 'aim'? Write your own definition in the activity box:

Activity 4.4

An aim is:

We need to have some overall sense of purpose or direction before we can think about the precise nature of the learning that is to take place. We need to consider in broad terms what **we, as teachers**, are trying to achieve. This is how we arrive at the aims of our sessions.

Aims then relate to an overall view of sessions or programmes and help us to answer questions like:

- What is the general purpose of this session or programme?
- Why am I delivering this teaching?
- Why is it worth me including this content in the session or programme?

If you were to ask us why we produced this book, our reply would be 'Because it will be useful to teachers'. You might then probe further, 'Why will it be useful to teachers?' Our response this time would be 'To provide a broad introduction to the theory and the practical side of teaching', or perhaps 'To support professionals wanting to gain a PTLLS award'. This would be our **aim**. As you can see, this statement or aim provides a compass setting, so that we have a general idea of the direction in which we wish to travel.

Sometimes it helps to ask additional questions such as:

- 'Why is this teaching worthwhile?'

or

- 'What am I trying to achieve?'

and keep asking, until the answer really expresses, in a concise statement, what you, as the teacher, want to achieve.

Consider the examples in the following illustration.

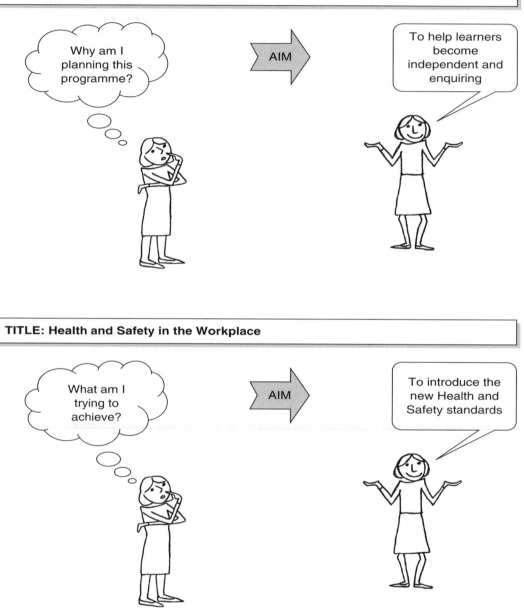

It can therefore be seen that:

An aim is a statement of what the teacher intends the general purpose and direction of the teaching programme should be.

Think now about a programme with which you are involved, or plan to be involved, or maybe a session you are to teach. What do you consider you want to achieve? What is your overall aim or aims?

Activity 4.5

Title of your course or teaching session:

Aims:

Clear aims are vital to give purpose and direction to your planning, but are not specific enough to give details of the actual route. At a more specific level we will now need to think about **learning objectives**.

Before we move on to writing learning objectives, let us think about what is meant by the term 'learning objective'. Write your own definition in the activity box:

Activity 4.6

A learning objective is:

We consider a learning objective to be 'a statement that defines the learning that is going to take place'. The more specific we can be about this learning, the more effective our planning will be. The box at the beginning of each chapter in this book lists the learning objectives for that chapter; it tells you what you will be learning. This is the first important characteristic of a learning objective. It describes the change that learning will bring about; what it is the learner will be able to do that they may not have been able to do before. Consider two of the learning objectives for this chapter:

- Define and distinguish between aims and learning objectives
- Write clear aims and learning objectives for teaching sessions

We hope you will agree they both describe what you will be learning as part of this chapter by identifying what you will now be able to do that you could not do before, assuming that this chapter contains new material or a new way of thinking about things.

Does each of the learning objectives above, however, suggest the same sorts of change? To help you decide, look at the learning objectives listed below, selected from various teaching courses. How do learning objectives 1, 4 and 5 differ from 2, 3 and 6?

At the end of this teaching session each learner will be able to:

1   State three factors influencing radio reception in hilly areas
2   Plant out seedlings
3   Ride a bicycle safely in a straight line for a distance of 100 metres
4   List ten countries which are currently members of the United Nations
5   State the prime numbers between 0 and 100 in ascending order
6   Construct a T joint from two pieces of wood

Activity 4.7

What sort of change or new learning is described in learning objectives 1, 4 and 5?

What sort of change or new learning is described in learning objectives 2, 3 and 6?

The answers you gave should indicate that learning objectives 1, 4 and 5 are concerned with acquiring knowledge, whereas learning objectives 2, 3 and 6 are to do with acquiring a skill.

Some learning objectives, then, will identify the learning that is to take place in terms of what we now **know** that we did not know before. Other learning objectives do so in terms of what we can now **do** that we could not do before. Sometimes, however, the type of change you will be aiming to bring about in your learners may be less to do with actual knowledge or skills than to do with the **value** they place on these. Your learning objective would then concern attitudes.

Learning objectives therefore fall into three different categories or 'domains'. These are:

1   Knowledge (also referred to as 'cognitive')
2   Skills (also referred to as 'psycho-motor')
3   Attitudes (also referred to as 'affective')

Here are two more learning objectives:

1 At the end of the session each learner will be able to list the five characteristics of a well-written learning objective.
2 At the end of the session each learner will know the letters of the Greek alphabet.

If you were expert in both these subjects, which of these learning objectives would you find the easier to plan part of a session around?

Activity 4.8

I would prefer to use learning objective ___ for planning because:

The problem with learning objective ___ is that it is:

You will probably agree that learning objective 1 is the most useful because it describes exactly the outcome we want, whereas learning objective 2 is too vague and ambiguous. After all, what does 'know' the Greek alphabet mean? Does it mean that the learner should be able to:

• Identify all the letters of the Greek alphabet?
• Write all the letters?
• Recall all the letters?
• Recite all the letters?
• Recite all the letters in the correct order?

In each case we are specifying different learning. From our original learning objective, 'know the Greek alphabet', any of these interpretations is acceptable, which makes the outcome uncertain. Learning objectives, then, must be written in a specific manner leading to a common interpretation.

Our other problem with the learning objective 'know the Greek alphabet' is that we will be uncertain whether it has been achieved. If we are not sure exactly what learning is to take place, how can we test it? This is the problem with 'knowing'. It is a process that takes place in learners' heads. We cannot see or hear what goes on inside heads so we need to express the learning in such a way that we can see or hear whether or not it has taken place; the evidence of learning lies in the actions learners now perform that they could not perform before learning took place. The second characteristic of learning objectives, then, is that they should be written in such a manner as to be measurable and this is achieved by use of an 'action verb'.

Activity 4.9

In the table below, pick out the examples of good action verbs for writing learning objectives.

define	select	understand	list
realise the significance of	measure	have a good grasp of	justify
really know	construct	label	be aware of
solve	be familiar with	demonstrate	distinguish between
describe	recall	explain	know
think	perform	appreciate	state
prepare	give reasons	report	be acquainted with

For solution, see p. 66.

A useful word to help you remember the characteristics of a well-written learning objective is **SMART**. The letters of this mnemonic (memory aid) stand for:

Specific

Measurable

Achievable

Relevant

Timed

Specific

The learning objective should describe the desired learning **exactly**, stating clearly what the learner will be able to do as a result of your teaching. To achieve this, care should be taken in choosing the appropriate **action verb**. The action verb is the word that comes immediately after *'will be able to ...'*.

Measurable

What the learner will be able to do should be observable. It should result in some form of action that allows you to satisfy yourself that learning has indeed taken place. This may be through listing, naming, explaining, recognising, demonstrating, performing or a number of other different ways in which the learners will show you they *'are able to ...'*.

Achievable

Regardless of how well your learning objective is written – it may be a model of clarity and clearly measurable – it is only of practical use if it is within the capabilities of the intended learners and sufficiently challenging. Learning objectives must be written with the learners in mind, which is why it is important to find out as much as you can about your learners prior to planning. After all it is they who *'will be able to ...'*.

Relevant

What is the point of this learning described by your learning objective? If the learners cannot see why it is important or how it will help them, then they may ask themselves why they should bother *'to be able to ...'*.

Time bound

How long will it take to achieve this learning objective? It may take one session, a week or a lifetime of trying. Learners should be made aware of how long it will be before they can be reasonably expected *'to be able to ...'*.

Learning objectives therefore allow us to:

- Identify clearly the learning that is to take place
- Make appropriate choices of methods and resources
- Select assessment strategies

Whichever type of objective you will be writing – knowledge, skill or attitude – you will need to ensure these are SMART.

Choosing appropriate methods

We can view teaching methods or learning activities in much the same way as a carpenter, a plumber or an electrician considers the tools in their toolbox. There will be a variety of tools to allow all sorts of tasks to be tackled. The most appropriate tools are selected after the task has been seen and before work commences. Similarly, as teachers, we have a range of methods and activities at our disposal and our skill lies in choosing the most appropriate method for the circumstances in which we find ourselves and then using that method effectively.

The factors that influence our choice of activity/method fall into three categories:

1   The learning that is to take place   – the **objectives**
2   Those who will undertake the learning   – the **learners**
3   The conditions in which the learning will take place   – the **reality factor**

The objectives

It is evident that we would **not** use particular teaching methods for some objectives. We would not, for instance, be wise to use the lecture method if we want learners to develop a skill, such as tying a knot to secure a boat to a post. Role play would be equally inappropriate to explain the workings of a car engine. It would be difficult to hold a discussion on something strictly factual, like the calculation of the area of a building. It is relatively easy to identify methods we would **not** use, but where do we start in deciding what methods we **do** use? It is apparent that the methods we associate with different subject specialisms stem from the type of learning or learning objectives associated with that subject.

There is some agreement at a basic level that certain activities are more appropriate for certain objectives. These are summarised below:

- Teaching methods appropriate to **knowledge** objectives include: lecture, brainstorm, games, project, and question and answer
- Methods that support the acquisition of **skills** include demonstration, practical exercise and simulation
- Methods appropriate for **attitude** objectives include discussion, games, role play and tutorial

Use the information from the lists above in the next activity.

 ## Activity 4.10

Select an appropriate teaching method from the list above to achieve the following learning objectives:

Learning objective

At the end of the teaching session each learner will be able to:

1   State three factors influencing flooding of the River Thames
2   Perform a forward somersault from a standing position
3   Ride a bicycle safely in a straight line for a distance of 100 metres
4   List four countries that became members of the European Community in 2007
5   Recognise the need for protective footwear on a construction site

6 Give four reasons for the increase in obesity in the UK
7 Recognise the importance of teamwork
8 Evaluate the pros and cons of developing renewable energy
9 Lead a walking bus to school
10 List the prime numbers between 0 and 100 in ascending order

Having made these links, you will appreciate that a key consideration in choosing an appropriate method is the objective that is to be achieved and whether it relates to knowledge, skills or attitudes.

The choice of tool is sometimes also evident from the nature of the task itself, and similarly within our different subject specialisms there are methods and activities on which we rely more than others. Chapters 6, 7 and 8 are concerned with thinking about the teaching of your subject specialism and the knowledge, skills and attitudes that learners need to acquire.

The learners

There are, however, further considerations to be made before arriving at a final decision; whilst the method we choose may fit the objective, it may **not** suit the learner or learners who will be achieving this objective. In Chapter 5 we look at the characteristics of learners that may also have a bearing on our choice of teaching method. Ultimately our choice of method must be one that accommodates both the objective and the learners. Whilst the lecture, for instance, may be an appropriate method for a knowledge objective, we would not use it with a lively group with short attention spans. Instead, we may well opt for a game, which would still be appropriate in achieving the objective but would also engage this particular group of learners.

The reality factor

Our third factor, reality, includes practical considerations such as:

• The time available
• The time of day or year
• The size of the group
• The space in which we will teach them
• The resources that are available to us
• How confident we are in the use of a particular method or resource

Thinking about these three factors – our objectives, our learners and our context – will help us to make the best choice of methods and ensure that we provide our learners with appropriate learning opportunities.

Chapter summary

The main points covered in this chapter are:

✓ Planning a session will make our delivery more effective and save effort next time round
✓ Learners should be the first consideration in planning a session
✓ Aims describe the teacher's general purpose
✓ Objectives define the learning that an individual will achieve
✓ Objectives relate to knowledge, skill or attitude and should be SMART – specific, measurable, achievable, relevant and time-bound
✓ To choose an appropriate method we need to consider the objective, the learner and the 'reality factor'

Solution to Activity 4.9

In the table below, the good action verbs for writing learning objectives are shown in **bold**

define	**select**	understand	**list**
realise the significance of	**measure**	have a good grasp of	**justify**
really know	**construct**	**label**	be aware of
solve	be familiar with	**demonstrate**	**distinguish between**
describe	**recall**	**explain**	know
think	**perform**	appreciate	**state**
prepare	**give reasons**	**report**	be acquainted with

📖 Further reading

Gray, D., Griffin, C. and Nasta, T. (2000) *Training to Teach in Further and Adult Education*. London: Stanley Thornes.
Chapter 4 on 'Curriculum Planning and Design' discusses aims and objectives and how to write these. Note how each chapter in this book starts.

Petty, G. (2004) *Teaching Today*, (3rd Edn). Cheltenham: Nelson Thornes.
Chapter 37 'Aims and Objectives' contains a full discussion and distinguishes between different types of objectives.

Kerry, T. (1999) *Effective Learning Objectives, Task-Setting and Differentiation*. London: Hodder and Stoughton.
An easy to read book which covers all of the areas highlighted in the title and illustrates the relationship between learning objectives and methods, assessment and evaluation.

Useful websites

www.tss.uoguelph.ca/resources/idres/learningobjectives1.pdf

http://usagso-sg.tripod.com/22_learning_objectives.pdf

5

Planning for individual learners

Chapter overview

When you have worked through this chapter on planning for individual learners you will be able to:

- Recognise the importance of initial assessment
- Identify individual differences and ways in which each may impact on learning
- Promote inclusion
- Select appropriate differentiation strategies
- Define equality and diversity
- Develop equality and diversity guidelines for your own teaching context

---

This chapter looks at issues of diversity, inclusion, differentiation and equality. Before you begin to work your way through it, reflect upon what these different terms mean.

 Activity 5.1

Define the following terms in your own words:

1 Diversity

2 Inclusion

3 Differentiation

4 Equality

You may want to revisit these definitions as you reach appropriate parts of the chapter. Before focusing on these interrelated issues we need to consider the individual nature of learners in the lifelong learning sector.

Initial assessment of learners

In Chapter 4 on planning, we found out how to write learning objectives in a way that ensures they will be both specific and measurable. An indication of the time in which we would expect the objective to be achieved was given by prefacing each action by the phrase 'by the end of the session each learner will be able to ...'. This covers S, M and T in the 'SMART' mnemonic (memory aid). But how do we make our objectives A (achievable, yet challenging) and R (relevant)?

Achievable and Relevant refer to learners. No matter how technically well written an objective, it is of little practical use if it does not take into account the nature and characteristics of the learners who are to achieve it. Learners in the lifelong learning sector come with a range of previous experiences and a wide range of different backgrounds and we can be certain that each group of learners we come across will possess different characteristics from another. Perhaps more importantly, the individuals within the group will each be different, as will their needs and talents.

Recognition of individual differences and needs starts from the moment that learners apply for courses. It is usual to organise an initial interview to make sure that the course applied for matches the learner's aspirations and capabilities. The most effective way we can ensure success is to make sure that learners' individual starting points have been taken into account and that they are on the appropriate course in the first place.

This is the first function of **initial assessment**. As such it begins with an examination of the qualifications that learners already hold. These will provide an indication of the level of skills or knowledge already achieved and allow some prediction to be made as to the likelihood of success if the learner is accepted onto the course. A judgement can also be made as to the level of course – foundation, intermediate, advanced – that is best for the particular learner.

Learners may have the appropriate prior learning and have identified a course of the appropriate level, but is the choice of course compatible with their needs, aspirations, interests and career goals? It may be that a purely academic course has been selected when a more vocational choice would better meet their needs. So choice needs to be discussed at an informal interview where all the possibilities can be examined to make sure that the final choice of course is both appropriate and well informed.

Having successfully placed learners on a course that is appropriate to their abilities and goals, the next function of initial assessment is to identify any kind of additional support that learners may need in order to successfully complete their chosen course of study. Learners may well have different levels of reading, writing, numeracy, language and ICT skills, all of which are crucial in any course that is undertaken, regardless of subject or level. Some adult learners may have attained Maths and English qualifications many years ago. It is likely that such qualifications may no longer give an accurate indication of levels of performance, perhaps due to lack of practice, or the nature of the skills required may have changed in the intervening years.

Diagnostic tests are normally undertaken by all learners in FE to ascertain their competence in these 'key' skills and identify the possible need for additional support. Learning difficulties, such as dyslexia, can also be identified at this stage. Again, appropriate arrangements can be made for the additional support learners will require in order to cope with the demands of their chosen course. The second function of initial assessment then, is to remove barriers to learning by identifying these at the beginning of the learner's course and to put into place the necessary arrangements to successfully manage them. The process can be taken further by identifying learning styles, making learners aware of their own approaches to learning and introducing them to strategies suited to their own preferences as well as enabling them to deal with situations that favour other approaches.

Most institutions within the lifelong learning sector will have specialists who carry out diagnostic testing, but the results of initial assessments should be made available to teachers and should inform Individual Learning Plans.

As part of the PTLLS course, you can expect to undertake initial assessment in literacy, numeracy and ICT. This is related to the need for you to evidence Level 2 performance in these areas in order to gain QTLS status. The results will identify your current level of competency and make you aware of what, if anything, you have to do to reach the required level. If you carry on to either CTLLS or DTLLS, addressing your personal skills in these areas will certainly form part of your Individual Learning Plan and action planning.

Individual differences

It is important to recognise the differences in the learners we teach as these may influence how we interact with them. To act professionally as teachers we will want to ensure that we behave in ways acceptable to all our learners, taking into account factors such as race, gender, age, previous experience or background.

Consider the learners with whom you have had contact so far or alternatively groups of learners of which you have been a part. What differences have you noticed?

 Activity 5.2

Write down some differences you have noticed in learners you have met:

The differences you have listed above all have implications for the way in which we teach, as each will affect that individual's learning and how we as teachers view that individual. We would not, however, want these differences to lower the expectations we have of any of our learners. Such expectations can be, sometimes unwittingly, transmitted in what we say and how we behave, and this can negatively affect the learning environment we provide for our learners.

Some of the typical individual differences you might encounter are listed below. Each of these may have its own particular effect on teaching and learning:

Age	Physical disability	Mental health issues
Cultural differences	Motivation	Religion
Ethnicity	Attention span	Previous experience
Gender	Personality	Aptitude
Sexual orientation	Learning difficulty	Learning styles

Pick **two** of your entries from Activity 5.2 and in the next activity describe how each of these characteristics may affect learning. Then decide how you might take this into account when teaching that individual.

Activity 5.3

Characteristic 1:

Possible effect on learning:

How might you take account of this in teaching a learner with this characteristic?

Characteristic 2:

Possible effect on learning:

How might you take account of this in teaching a learner with this characteristic?

As an example, consider the different ways in which we prefer to take in information. When we learn, some of us prefer to take in information through words (either written or spoken), others prefer visual means (pictures, diagrams), whilst others like to engage directly with the information and learn through 'doing'. Although most learners will be able to use several techniques, some will find difficulties and frustrations when engaging in techniques that do not match their preferred style.

Suppose you get a new computer. You might take it out of the box and try to assemble it and get it to work straight away by looking at all the different parts and trying to work out which bit connects together. You would do this because your preferred way of accessing information and subsequently learning is through 'doing'. If you got stuck, however, and could not make it work, you might well unpack the instruction manual and either read through what it says or look at the diagrams it contains for guidance. You might not have looked at the manual first of all, not because you could not understand it, but because your natural preference is to learn through 'doing'. Someone else might start by reading the manual or by looking at the diagrams because that is their preference. One model of categorising individual preferences is 'VAK' – visual, aural, kinaesthetic (for more details, see www.vak-learn.co).

In any group of learners we meet, it is likely that we will encounter this mix of preferences for taking in information. We could conduct our teaching session by talking and explaining to learners, supporting this by slides with the appropriate definitions and summaries of the main points. After all, most people are capable of taking in some information from words.

An alternative would be to talk and explain to learners supported by slides with pictures and diagrams of what we are explaining and then follow this up with some exercises where learners use the information we are trying to put across to them.

In this second approach, we would be trying to ensure that at some stage in the session we catered for each of the different ways of accessing information – we would be trying to ensure that all, and not just some learners, were being accommodated. If we had done an individual analysis of preferred styles we would also be aware at which point the approach might best suit each individual learner.

 ## Activity 5.4

Think of a topic you teach through words only. What else might you do with this topic to suit all learners and the ways in which they prefer to take in information?

Diversity

The above discussion illustrates a number of concepts that are considered to be of great importance within lifelong learning. The range of differences encountered within any group of learners is referred to as **diversity**. The following definition is quoted by Clements and Jones (2006: 13):

> **Diversity is defined by 'otherness' or those human qualities that are different from our own and outside the groups to which we belong, yet are present in other individuals or groups. (University of Maryland, 1995)**

Another way of defining diversity is 'Different Individuals Valuing Each other Regardless of Skin, Intellect, Talent or Years' (www.trendenterprises.com). A poster with these words, spelling out Diversity, can be seen on the walls of many lifelong learning establishments to raise awareness of the diversity in the learner population.

Inclusion

Diversity brings richness to the group and provides a wealth of previous experience and contribution that might not otherwise exist. A possible consequence, however, is that some learners will feel excluded as their particular needs are not being met. If we are to be effective in our teaching, all learners should feel part of and engaged in the particular session. If this is the case, our approach would be said to be demonstrating **inclusion**.

Inclusion operates at many different levels and in many different contexts. In 1996 Tomlinson defined inclusion as 'the greatest degree of match or fit between individual learning requirements and provision'. The major concern of his report was the 'inclusion' of students with learning difficulties and disabilities in mainstream college provision, but from a more general viewpoint we can consider inclusive teaching as teaching that allows **all** learners to potentially benefit and learn from any aspect of a teaching session. Inclusion is both about planning so that all learners are included and also about learners **feeling** included.

Differentiation

The strategies we use to ensure inclusion in the learning environment/teaching context are collectively known as **differentiation** strategies.

Activity 5.5

List any differentiation strategies you have experienced as a learner or used in your teaching sessions:

When introducing material to a whole group, a variety of methods can be used to take account of the different preferred learning styles, attitudes and motivation of individual learners within the group. Presentation methods may differentiate in terms of learners accessing the material, as previously explained, but they are teacher-led and may not sufficiently take account of the different levels of understanding or previous experience learners have within the particular topic.

Activities that encourage learners to use and process the information are much more successful in allowing individuals to engage in learning at an appropriate level. Generally, the more open an activity and the more you give control to learners, the more the level is self-regulated and learning occurs at a manageable but challenging level for each individual. It can be argued that, given the opportunity, learners themselves manage differentiation more effectively than teachers. Open activities are not always possible, however, and as teachers we can use a number of different strategies to achieve a more differentiated and inclusive approach to teaching and learning.

Differentiation can be achieved in a number of different ways:

1   Within any group that you teach, there may well be individual learners with specific needs relating to some form of learning difficulty or disability. Institutions have different methods of requesting that learners self-disclose any learning difficulty or disability on enrolment and will then normally provide support, such as hearing loops or signers for hearing-impaired learners, adaptive software for visually impaired learners and scribes/software for those learners with communication difficulties such as severe dyslexia. Organisations such as AbilityNet can supply enabling resources. These can be supplemented by simpler 'teacher-initiated' measures such as a consideration of seating positions, clear enunciation, enlarged print on handouts and other written material, use of coloured paper (different colours suit individual learners) and appropriate fonts (Comic Sans font on blue paper, for instance, may be helpful for some learners with dyslexia).

   Despite your best efforts you may not be fully aware of all those within your group who have a learning difficulty or disability as this is to a large extent dependent on learner self-disclosure. This can make it difficult for the teacher to identify and respond with the appropriate support. Irregular attendance, for example, can be caused by mental health issues which learners may choose not to disclose. If you, as a teacher, are aware of the issue it is easier to propose adjustments.

2   If we set a single learning objective for a whole group, it is likely that it will not be appropriate for all learners, as whilst it may be achievable by the majority, it may be too easy or too difficult for others, due to the diversity of the group. At this stage it is useful to look at the classic work of Benjamin Bloom (1956), who, in his *Taxonomy of Objectives*, introduced the idea of different levels of performance. If a learning objective is concerned with knowledge, for instance, Bloom identified six different levels of performance:

- Knowledge – being able to recall or recognise the material to be learned
- Comprehension – understanding the learned material
- Application – putting the learned material to use
- Analysis – breaking down the learned material and drawing conclusions
- Synthesis – using the learned material to form new ideas
- Evaluation – using the learned material to make judgements, present and defend opinions

If we apply this to a physics lesson on electricity, we could write the following learning objective:

- By the end of this session each learner will be able to describe the differences between a series and a parallel circuit

This is an objective that looks for Comprehension and may be appropriate for most, but if applied to a diverse group may be too difficult for some and too easy for others. One possibility in this situation is to have supplementary objectives, one of which might be at a lower level of Bloom's Taxonomy, looking only for Knowledge:

- By the end of this session each learner will be able to identify examples of series and parallel circuits

and one of which might address the next higher level, of Application:

- By the end of this session each learner will be able to decide whether a series or parallel circuit is appropriate for a given situation

Although the group as a whole might be covering the same topic, learning is personalised so that different outcomes can be achieved within it, ensuring all learners succeed and are challenged. We can achieve this through group work using graduated tasks or worksheets, or by supplying extra resource material as required. So, you can achieve differentiation through setting different levels of learning objective.

3   We may decide to have learners working either individually or in groups on the same learning outcome. Some may finish earlier than others and some may find difficulty in completing the task. Our problem is to keep those who have finished early occupied and stretched whilst having time to give extra

assistance to those who need it. To give the early finishers 'more of the same' is not the best option. Instead, you can have an 'extension task' ready and you simply tell learners what this is at the appropriate time, or have it available in written form. An extension task covers the same content but takes learners up to the next level of Bloom's Taxonomy. If the original learning objective was at the 'Knowledge' level, the extension task would take learners up to the 'Comprehension' level and so on. You can then take feedback at the end of the activity, which incorporates the extension task as well as the original learning objective.

4   When setting up group work, we can think carefully about the composition of the group. If, for instance, we have a fairly diverse group as a whole, how can we ensure that when we break them up into smaller groups, we are creating a differentiated environment? One possibility is to group learners by expertise. The more expert groups can get on with the task giving us the time to spend with those learners who are in most need of it. On the other hand, we can form groups with a spread of expertise with the more expert members of the group providing support to those who need to develop further. We can then be more responsive to the moment in terms of allocating our attention. There may well be other possibilities that provide better differentiation, depending upon the needs of the particular group and the individual learners within it, but the point is that the setting up of group work provides an opportunity to ensure a differentiated approach. If you place learners in different groups for different tasks they can work with a wider range of people and increase their feeling of inclusion – although this will only happen if a positive social environment is created within which learners feel confident to learn.

5   Directed questioning can also provide a route to a differentiated approach. Simpler questions would be directed to less confident learners and more challenging supplementary questions could be directed towards learners who need to be stretched.

6   The most personalised approach to meeting individual needs within a diverse group is to set individual objectives and tasks on an individual learning plan. This can be achieved within a workshop or project setting where learners work independently from each other. When you reach Chapter 12 on planning, you will see that the planning format for workshops encourages the setting of individual objectives and monitoring progress at an individual level. Potentially, learners can become involved in the setting of their own objectives.

   The best way to examine your practice with respect to differentiation is to look back after teaching a session and analyse what you did and what the learners thought of it (Chapter 13 on evaluation provides some useful guidance on self-evaluation). If you are at all sensitive to the needs of your learners, you will undoubtedly find that although you may not have planned it or even realised that you were doing it, you will have differentiated in some manner and have involved learners in this process. Recognising this is the first step to becoming more aware of the issue and beginning to differentiate in a more systematic and deliberate manner. Another possibility is to observe another teacher and spot any strategies they may have used or, alternatively, reflect back on your own learning and identify occasions on which you felt truly 'included'.

Activity 5.6

Identify at least two new differentiation strategies you could use in your teaching:

Equality

Inclusion is very much related to issues of **equality**. Within the context of lifelong learning, equality is considered to encompass:

- An expectation of fair treatment
- An opportunity to participate on equal terms

Activity 5.7

Does equality mean we should treat all learners in the same manner or differently? Why and what examples can you provide?

An expectation of fair treatment requires us as teachers to be non-judgemental and accept that people see the world differently and that these world-views have equal validity. We need not agree with all opinions that are expressed, and may well wish to challenge and debate some of them, but this does not mean that we do not recognise the right of our learners to hold different opinions. This aspect of equality and diversity requires us to value and treat all learners fairly, in the same consistent manner, 'without fear or favour', with dignity and respect. We would doubtless all claim to do this, but it is inevitable that our views of learners will be subject to some bias – we are only human after all.

The section on reliability in assessment (see Chapter 10) illustrates how difficult it is to adopt a totally non-judgemental, accepting position towards all learners, whether we are aware of it or not. Other issues such as stereotyping of learners and presenting stereotypical views to learners also come into play here. We need to be aware of our own prejudices and how these shape our behaviour, especially as in our role as teachers our behaviour can shape the attitudes and behaviours of our learners.

The second aspect of equality acknowledges that we recognise learners do not all start from the same point and we need to take account of this in our planning. The institution that you work in will have a policy related to Equality and Diversity to address such matters (some institutions have separate policies relating to race, gender and disability whilst others hold these in a single equality scheme).

Examples of institutional support include crèche facilities provided for learners with need for childcare; and bursaries available for those for whom finance represents a barrier to access. At the level of individual teaching sessions, equality of access can be a key issue. Ramps and lifts may be provided for learners with a physical disability or classes timetabled in ground floor accommodation to ensure that 'reasonable adjustments' are made. Within a teaching session, similar barriers may exist – access to resources, access to the teacher's time and support, for instance – and we need to be aware of these.

Activity 5.8

Devise Equality and Diversity guidelines for the sessions that you teach:

Initial assessment may have identified those who require additional support with areas such as literacy or numeracy. Most institutions will provide additional learning support either on an individual or group basis as well as a number of other kinds of student support designed to allow all learners to compete on equal terms.

It can be seen that issues of diversity, equality and inclusion permeate the teaching and learning process and operate at all different levels – individual, group, institution and society. These issues will need to be kept in mind as you read the next chapters on methods for teaching different subject specialisms.

Chapter summary

The main points covered in this chapter are:

✓ Initial assessment establishes that learners are on the most appropriate courses to meet their individual needs and, where necessary, suitable arrangements for additional support can be made quickly and effectively

✓ Learners in the lifelong learning sector exhibit a wide range of individual differences which can influence the ways in which learning takes place. Diversity is the term used to describe this range of differences

✓ Inclusion is the process whereby **all** learners are made to feel part of the learning process

✓ Differentiation is the term used to describe the strategies used to achieve an inclusive approach

✓ Differentiation can be achieved in a number of ways, such as setting learning objectives at different levels and using extension tasks

✓ Equality involves the fair and consistent treatment of learners, whilst ensuring equality of opportunity in participating in learning

✓ All of the above issues operate at national, institutional, group and individual levels

→ References

Bloom, B. (1956) *Taxonomy of Educational Objectives: Handbook 1*. New York: Longman.

Clements, P. and Jones, J. (2006) *The Diversity Training Handbook*, (2nd Edn). London: Kogan Page.

University of Maryland (1995) www.inform.umd.edu.

Tomlinson, J. (1996) Report of the *Further Education Funding Council Learning Difficulties and/or Disabilities Committee*. Coventry: FEFC.

Further reading

Kerry, T. (1999) *Effective Learning Objectives, Task-Setting and Differentiation*. London: Hodder and Stoughton.

An easy to read book with a variety of strategies that can be used to differentiate.

Race, P. (2005) *Making Learning Happen: A Guide for Post-Compulsory Education*. London: Sage Publications.

Chapter 8 discusses the changing nature of learners in post compulsory education and gives detail on specific special needs.

Petty, G. (2004) *Teaching Today – A Practical Guide*, (3rd Edn). Cheltenham: Nelson Thornes.

A useful overview of several different aspects of diversity with checklists against which to compare your own practice. For an interesting account of the relationship between stereotyping and equality, see Chapter 7.

Useful websites

Differentiation

http://members.shaw.ca/priscillatheroux/differentiatingstrategies.html

http://members.shaw.ca/priscillatheroux/differentiating.html

Equality and diversity

www.equalityhumanrights.com includes information and further links on ethnicity and race, disability and gender

www.lsneducation.org.uk. This site contains a range of national guidance and publications, for example, 'The Disability Discrimination Act – Do you have a disability, yes or no? Or is there a better way of asking' Christine Rose

Inclusion

http://inclusion.ngfl.gov.uk/

http://ctl.unc.edu/tfi2.html

How to teach theory

Chapter overview

When you have worked through this chapter on the teaching of theory you will be able to:

■ **Identify methods to use in helping learners acquire theory or knowledge**
■ **Recognise the strengths and limitations of lecturing**
■ **Develop strategies to deliver an effective lecture**
■ **Distinguish between active and passive learning**
■ **Use different approaches to questioning**
■ **Deal effectively with answers to questions**

Ultimately we want the learners we teach to be able to use what they have learned in a meaningful way. Before reaching the 'using' stage, however, there is a certain amount of knowledge or theory that has to be acquired.

Some subjects are considered more 'theoretical' than others. If you teach in Higher Education, 'AS' or 'A' level courses for instance, you may well consider your subject as falling within this category; but every subject, regardless of level, has its own body of knowledge and its own underpinning theory upon which its practice relies. For example:

• When learning about accountancy, a knowledge of 'debit' and 'credit' must be gained prior to beginning to 'balance the books'
• A knowledge of the different types of bonding is required before learners can begin to construct a brick wall
• Before trying to diagnose why a car will not start, a sound knowledge of the theory of combustion and electrical circuits is essential if an accurate diagnosis is to be achieved
• A knowledge of perspective is required before drawing up a garden design

In this chapter we will be considering how best to present such knowledge and theory to our learners.

The lecture

Traditionally, the lecture has been used for the purpose of teaching theory or knowledge. The term 'lecture' is normally associated with one person passing on information to many people seated in rows in a 'lecture theatre'. It is a process that is relatively independent of learner reaction or participation. In this chapter, a looser definition is used, which includes:

> **any talk-based activity which serves the purpose of conveying information in a structured manner to a group of learners.**

In the vast majority of cases within lifelong learning, any session will consist of a variety of different types of activity and it is unlikely that a whole session will be devoted to delivering information. There will be times, however, when sizeable chunks of factual material have to be put across and it is such occasions that we seek to address in this chapter.

For convenience we will continue to use the term 'lecture', although the modern version of the lecture will be conducted in a relatively relaxed rather than formal atmosphere, with seating arrangements that may encourage all-round communication. As such, however, it still possesses a number of positive features that characterise what we think of as a traditional lecture.

- The desired material can be imparted to a large number of people in a fairly short period of time
- The pace at which, and the sequence in which, material is delivered can be controlled for maximum efficiency
- Information is up-to-date and accurate
- Learners can be enthused and encouraged to explore the topic further

Despite the above, the lecture is often held in low regard.

 Activity 6.1

What drawbacks do you see with the lecture approach?

One definition of a lecture is 'the process by which the notes of the professor become the notes of the student without ever passing through the mind of either', and it has been suggested that a lecturer is 'someone who talks in other people's sleep'. The lecture, however, has stood the test of time. It has been around in one form or another since Greek times and is still used extensively in many lifelong learning contexts, although it may be redefined as 'explanation', 'verbal exposition' or 'direct instruction'.

There is an argument to suggest that the problems associated with the lecture are more to do with poor application than with the method itself and that a well-structured, well-delivered lecture can be most effective. As Brookfield (2006: 97) observes:

> Lecturing can certainly be done abominably. But just because something is done badly by some teachers in some classrooms does not mean the method as a whole is inherently flawed.

There are, however, a number of factors to be considered if we wish to deliver an effective lecture, which you will probably have identified in the previous activity. These relate largely to attention span, note-taking, active or passive learning and the potential absence of feedback.

Attention span

The most important aspect of learning that must be considered when using a lecture type of approach relates to the learners and how long they can concentrate on listening to a lecture. This is illustrated in Figure 6.1.

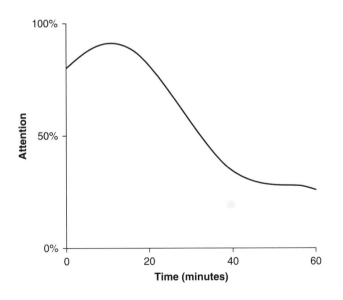

Figure 6.1

The curve in Figure 6.1 represents the way in which learner attention levels vary with time. It tells us that attention levels are high at the beginning of a period of learning, but fall away after a short period of time. What is of interest to us is the length of time for which that period of high attention is maintained. This will vary from learner to learner but the activity in which the learner engages is also significant and generally active methods hold attention for longer than passive methods.

When it comes to periods of uninterrupted talk by teachers, estimates of high attention levels vary from about 12 to 20 minutes. Lectures normally last for a longer period of time than this, but one way of overcoming the problem of attention span is to intersperse periods of teacher talk or lecture with short active learning activities, such as those you have identified in the exercise above. Each time we change the activity, the curve (and thus high attention levels) starts again (Figure 6.2).

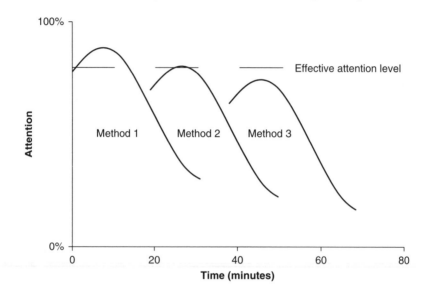

Figure 6.2

One of the reasons for short attention spans is to do with the way in which we take in information through the senses. As we will see in Chapter 9, sight is the sense upon which we are most reliant under normal circumstances. When we listen to uninterrupted talk, we have to rely solely on hearing. This is not natural and so involves a lot of hard work on our part to focus exclusively on the spoken word. We can only maintain this level of effort for a limited period of time. To relieve the burden on hearing the teacher can use visual aids, which bring our major sense, sight, back into play.

There is more than one way, then, to present the content of our lecture. We can tell our learners what they need to know but we can also **show** them: 'a picture paints a thousand words'. Visual aids, used appropriately, enhance a lecture by:

- Focusing attention on the important points and emphasising structure
- Creating interest and helping prolong concentration

- Making it easier to understand the material being presented
- Helping learners to remember information
- Giving our ears a rest!

In the following activity, think about how you can enhance your teaching of theory by use of visual aids. Chapter 9 will help give you some ideas in this respect.

 Activity 6.2

List the different visual aids you might use

Note taking

If you are reading a book, can you also watch television at the same time? You may well argue that this is indeed possible, but there would be parts of the TV programme that you would completely miss because, at that time, your attention was focused on your reading. Similarly your reading would be of a 'stop, start' nature as you periodically turned your attention to the television.

Generally, it is impossible to split or divide attention between two activities, particularly when, as in the above example, they involve the same sense. Because of the passive nature of the learning, we find it difficult to remember all of the information given in a lecture; we feel a need to take notes as the lecture progresses. Can we take notes and listen to the lecture at the same time, however? Well, yes, we can and do, but only if we divide our attention between the two. The result will be that we miss some of the content of the lecture because at that time our attention was focused on writing our notes or our notes will be incomplete because we were listening to the lecture!

Learners often produce rough notes and never refer to them; so do learners need notes? The necessity for notes will depend to some extent upon the complexity and familiarity of the content of the lecture. Learners can be encouraged to develop their own methods of effective note taking, such as using abbreviations, bullet points, numbers or perhaps recording notes in the form of questions. As teachers, we should also make a contribution to easing the burden of note taking.

Activity 6.3

How can we help learners to produce effective notes?

Strategies revolve around supplying either the notes themselves or a framework within which learners can produce their own notes, thus minimising divided attention and ensuring reasonable accuracy in the notes taken. Remember that learners have different preferences towards learning; the more visual may prefer to create mind maps, whilst the more verbal may find note taking helps them to process information.

It is possible to have a direct impact on note taking through the way in which we deliver information, particularly if we make learners aware in advance that we will:

- Avoid unnecessary note taking by highlighting main points visually
- Pause after the main points
- Summarise periodically, giving a few moments to record the point made

Active and passive learning

Passive learning involves learners only in receiving information, either verbally or visually. Active learning means that as well as receiving information, learners also actively engage with and use the material to be learned. The significance of the two categories can be seen in Figure 6.3, an adaptation of Dale's (1969) Cone of Learning. This suggests that we remember far less of what is presented to us when passive rather than active methods are used.

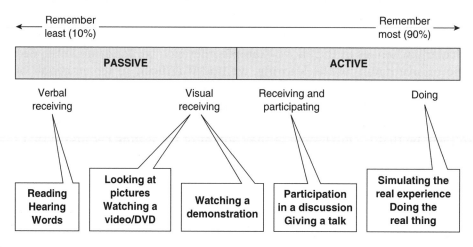

Figure 6.3

In a typical traditional lecture situation, students are often only passively involved in learning – listening to the teacher, looking at the occasional overhead or PowerPoint slide and taking notes. So, although a lecture can impart material to a large number of people in a short period of time, how much of it do they understand and subsequently remember? Very little it would appear, but according to Dale, the amount remembered would be increased considerably if we were to include episodes of active learning within our lecture.

Active learning involves 'doing' and thinking about the information presented and can include interaction with other students. Ideally, in the lecture situation this would involve fairly sharp, short exercises which would promote active learning without interrupting the flow of information too much.

Activity 6.4

List as many different short active learning exercises as you can think of which could be used to good effect in a lecture. You can compare your answers with the suggestions in the websites listed at the end of the chapter.

Your response to the exercise may have included activities like brainstorming, which requires a whole group response; or activities where learners work together in pairs or small 'buzz' groups, in which they have to complete short tasks that involve thinking about and using the information they have been given.

Learners could, for instance, be asked to give a two minute summary of the main points of the lecture to date to their neighbour who then has to report back one of those points to the group as a whole. Alternatively, a short, two sentence case study could be displayed using PowerPoint and a group of one pair and the pair sitting directly behind them could be asked to discuss the case study and arrive at a solution in five minutes. The teacher could then give the possible solutions, with a show of hands for agreement with each solution.

With a little imagination, a number of resources such as case studies, problem-solving exercises, multiple choice questions, diagrams or charts can be adapted to form the basis of short activities that learners can engage in singly, in pairs or small groups as part of the overall lecture. The characteristic they will all have in common is that they require learners to think about, take further or consolidate the information they receive in an active manner.

Feedback

The lecture often comes under fire for the lack of opportunity it affords for feedback, either to those giving the lecture or those receiving it. Lecturers cannot say with any confidence whether learners understand what is being presented to them and learners cannot be sure that their interpretation is in fact the correct one.

There are strategies that can be used to increase levels of understanding. The most obvious of these is to have a good knowledge of the learners – their previous knowledge and experience, their current levels of understanding, their aptitude for the subject. The way in which the required information is delivered can also make a significant difference to the way in which it is received.

Activity 6.5

How can we make the information we deliver easier to understand?

If we make information more 'real', easier to link with learners' previous experience and less abstract, it is generally easier to process. We can achieve this by:

- Starting explanations from a question
- Using real-life examples to introduce new concepts
- Quoting our own or learners' experiences
- Using case studies
- Using analogies to demonstrate relationships – for example, as used in the holiday journey in Chapter 4 on Planning
- Explaining 'jargon' before introducing the actual terminology
- Summarising sections of information and linking to the next section

Even if our lecture is a model of clarity, we still need some form of feedback to gauge its effectiveness. There are non-verbal cues, of course (posture, facial expressions, eye contact or the lack of it), but these can only give an impression and are often capable of misinterpretation. Some of the 'Active Learning' activities you have already suggested may be helpful in this respect, but are there other, more direct strategies that could be adopted?

Activity 6.6

How can we gain feedback as part of a lecture?

Many of the active learning techniques identified can provide useful, informal feedback. Direct questioning is another alternative but general questioning accompanied by some mechanism that allows all learners to respond is probably more effective as we shall see in the next section. The simplest way of obtaining feedback is by a 'show of hands' for agreement or disagreement with specific answers to questions, but this is rather limited.

Devices such as mini whiteboards provide a more informative take. These are small, hand-held whiteboards of approximately A4 size. Learners can write answers to questions asked by the teacher on the whiteboards using ordinary board markers and hold these up, thus giving an overview of answers from the group as a whole. The boards are then cleaned ready for further use. Variations on this theme include small, different coloured squares of card. These can be used to answer multiple choice questions, for instance, each possible response corresponding to a different colour. In response for feedback in general, red cards can indicate difficulty, green cards, understanding. Many creative solutions to the problem of lack of feedback are possible.

Invariably if you are helping learners to acquire theory you will be introducing new terminology and using the specialised language, concepts or 'jargon' of the subject or vocational area. Jargon is useful to us and at some stage it has to be learned so that we all 'speak the same language', particularly in a vocational context when all the learners will be doing the same job. The introduction of too much specialist language in a lecture, however, can be overwhelming and lead to learners 'switching off' or a general lack of understanding.

How much new terminology can be absorbed depends upon the nature of your group and the individuals within it. To get a feel for this, we need to be constantly checking learners' understanding. Engaging our learners in active learning methods gives them the opportunity to use the new language and can provide us with valuable feedback.

If your teaching requires you to deliver a considerable amount of factual or theoretical material, you may well use an approach based on the original notion of the lecture. If so, use the following checklist to make your presentation more effective:

Checklist for a lecture

☑ Have you checked the level of existing knowledge before you begin?

☑ Does your lecture have a logical structure? Does each point reinforce and build on previous points?

☑ Is your lecture reasonably short, using visual aids to maintain attention?

☑ Have you planned for learner participation by including active learning methods?

☑ Have you included some real-life examples and analogies to help understanding?

☑ Have you planned the introduction of specialist language carefully?

☑ Have you planned to summarise after key sections?

☑ Have you considered note taking?

☑ Are there opportunities for feedback?

Question and answer

The use of question and answer is another way of breaking up a 'lecture' and making it more active. You may well have used questioning in one form or another in your response to the earlier activity on active learning. Questioning by the teacher can accomplish a variety of different purposes; to use the technique effectively, the specific function of the question should be clear in the questioner's mind.

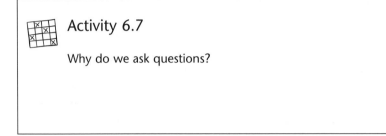

Activity 6.7

Why do we ask questions?

Your responses to the activity probably include:

- To test for existing knowledge. This could be finding out about what learners already know and bring to the session with them – important to know as you would wish to build upon this
- Alternatively you may wish to check if learners are acquiring the new knowledge you present to them – feedback to you the teacher
- To motivate learners by giving them the opportunity to demonstrate their learning, or alternatively making them aware of their learning – feedback to the learners
- To encourage participation and involvement in the session, important if you wish to promote Active Learning
- To use learners as a resource
- To build up knowledge step by step or guide learners towards the answers you require
- To stimulate curiosity and encourage thought
- To maintain attention
- To let learners know that you are interested in them and their views and that they can learn from each other by sharing these
- To encourage divergent thinking

An awareness of why we are asking questions is important, as our purpose will determine both the type of questions we ask and the way in which we ask them.

The skills in using question and answer technique fall into two parts:

1 Framing and asking questions
2 Dealing with the responses

Framing and asking questions

Whatever the type of questions we ask our learners, it is vitally important that they are clear and unambiguous. First we will look at closed questions and then consider those of a more open nature.

Sometimes we will be seeking specific information from learners; we may want to test their knowledge, focus attention on particular aspects of the skill in question or build up knowledge in a step-by-step fashion through questioning rather than telling. If this is the case, we will use **closed questions** that point the learner towards the desired response. This sounds simple enough, but in practice is not always that easy.

Closed questions have to be sufficiently narrow to give the learner some indication of the type of answer we are looking for. It may be that we do not get an answer to our question because the question is too general or vague rather than because learners do not know the answer. Equally, however, the question must not be so 'closed' that the answer is obvious and there is no challenge in providing it.

When using closed questions, we first identify the answer that we are looking for and then devise a question that will draw out this answer. When using a series of closed questions to build up knowledge, a similar approach is adopted. The information to be conveyed is first recorded in the correct order. A series of questions is then devised which will extract the appropriate answers in the desired order.

 ## Activity 6.8

Identify a subject you currently teach by 'telling'. Devise a series of closed questions that could be used to impart the same information.

Topic:

Information	Question to draw out information
1	
2	
3	
4	
5	
6	
7	
8	
9	
10	

On other occasions we may want to find out what the learner thinks, what their views and perceptions are, or we may wish them to consider an issue or come up with a variety of ideas around a specific topic. We may wish to initiate discussion, debate or divergent thinking. In this case we do not wish to guide learners towards a predetermined answer or indeed to influence their answer at all, but to allow them to think creatively and express themselves freely. In this case, **open questions** are much more appropriate. In this case we are likely to be posing questions that encourage learners to think more broadly about How? Why? Where? When? and What?

Once we have decided whether questions will be closed or open we need to consider which learners we want to answer the question. Will we encourage everyone to offer a response or direct specific learners to respond?

General questioning consists of asking questions of the group as a whole. You could consider this as non-threatening in its approach as learners have the option of answering or not. Whilst this sounds a good idea, the effectiveness of this approach can be questioned on a number of grounds:

- Less confident learners can be reluctant to participate
- More confident learners can dominate
- Individual responses can be missed by the group as a whole unless we repeat them
- We often make assumptions on behalf of the group as a whole based on the answers of individual learners

Many of these limitations can be overcome by the use of directed questions. Directed questioning involves the teacher nominating the person who is to answer thus allowing questions to be distributed around the group as a whole, giving all learners an opportunity to answer. This approach can and does 'put learners on the spot'. This does not, and indeed should not, mean this becomes a threatening or intimidating experience. It will only become so if the teacher is insensitive to the characteristics of their learners or misuses questioning to 'show up' learners for inattention or some other misdemeanour.

Directed questioning offers an opportunity for a differentiated approach. Learners can be asked specific questions that are within their ability to respond but still constitute a challenge. More able and confident learners can be asked more difficult or abstract questions whilst less able or less confident learners can be given less complex questions or questions that require them to recount an experience and be descriptive rather than analytical.

A good teacher will use their knowledge of their learners and their respective capabilities, taking account of body language, when deciding where to allocate a given question. If, during a question and answer session, a learner suddenly finds a speck of dust on their shoe or an unsightly mark on the ceiling that demands their attention, for instance, it might be better to direct that question to someone else!

An effective strategy for directed questions is the 'pose, pause, pounce and praise' sequence in which:

1 A general question is **posed** to the group as a whole, as if one learner is nominated to answer at this stage (pounce) the others will relax and 'switch off'. Posing a general question first invites the entire group to think about an answer.
2 A **pause** is allowed for consideration of the question. Learners are given thinking time to take in the questions and arrive at an answer. Teachers are given thinking time to scan the group and decide who this question is best directed towards.
3 The appropriate learner is named (**pounce**) and gives their answer
4 The teacher acknowledges the answer, giving **praise** as appropriate and repeating the answer to the rest of the group.

Whichever type of question we use, to be effective it should:

- Be reasonably short; effort can be put into arriving at an answer rather than trying to remember the question
- Contain only one idea; effort can be put into arriving at an answer rather than trying to work out which part needs answering
- Use language with which the learner is familiar; effort can be put into arriving at an answer rather than trying to decipher the question

Dealing with responses

Correct answers

This is the most straightforward case. A correct answer suggests that the question was well framed and within learners' capacity to answer. This is a situation we

> Well done John, that was an excellent answer. What John said was …

would like to encourage so we reward correct answers with acknowledgement and praise. It may be appropriate to repeat the answer to ensure everyone has heard. This also allows the opportunity to rephrase the answer a little to make sure it aids learning exactly as we want.

Partially correct answers

It is important here to first give credit for the part of the answer that is correct before going on to deal with the part that is incorrect. This can be achieved in a number of ways but perhaps the most effective is to ask if anyone wants to add to it. The appropriate response will normally then arise from other contributions. If no alternative explanation is forthcoming, we can offer it ourselves.

> Thank you, I liked the first part of your answer but I'm not sure about the second part. What do the rest of you think?

Incorrect answers

An incorrect answer can arise from a lack of knowledge, misinterpretation of the question or perhaps from the poor framing of the question itself. Whatever the reason, we don't wish to discourage learners from answering again. We therefore need to reply in a non-critical manner. Subsequent shorter closed questions could be asked to lead the learner to the required answer or the question could be redirected. We should not leave other learners in any doubt about the correct answer to our questions. To maintain the learner's confidence, they could be asked another question that we are confident they can answer, fairly soon afterwards.

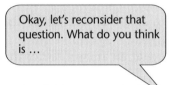

No answer at all

The lack of a response, even after redirecting, calls for a rephrasing of the question or breaking it down into smaller, simpler components. This will hopefully identify the cause of the lack of response. It may be that the subject of the question needs to be retaught, but alternatively it may be poor question framing that is the culprit. Avoid answering your own questions!

As a rule, it is best to repeat the responses to questions to the whole group. Quite often, not everyone hears what is said and repetition also gives us the opportunity to slightly rephrase or 'tweak' the answer received. Whatever you decide, the overriding principle is that all answers must receive a response of some kind!

Questioning is, of course, a two-way process and as well as asking questions, teachers can be on the receiving end and be required to provide the answers. This can be a worrying prospect for inexperienced teachers who anticipate they may be asked questions to which they do not know the answer. In reality, this is unlikely but on the odd occasion that it does happen, the secret is not to bluff.

Learners are far more accepting of teachers who admit to not knowing the answer (provided it does not happen on too regular a basis) than they are of teachers who pretend to know but obviously do not. A compliment on asking a good question and a promise to find out the answer is normally well received. Alternatively there may be expertise within the group that can be 'tapped into' by an open invitation to provide an answer.

You may occasionally be asked a question that would sidetrack learners; best then to propose discussing it with the individual learner during the break or at the end of the session and then making sure that you do. A more common issue is that of keeping the group as a whole involved when questions are asked on an individual basis. Redirecting the question back to the group is often effective in this instance.

Questioning then can be used in tandem with lectures to encourage participation and to maintain attention. As we have seen, however, as with all of the various methods and activities involved in teaching, it involves careful management to be effective, so here are some points to consider when using questioning:

☑ We should ask simple questions first to encourage responses and build confidence

☑ We should allow learners time to absorb the question and formulate a response

☑ We need to ensure all learners can hear both the question and the answer

☑ We should avoid asking questions of learners if we know they cannot answer. Eye contact, or the lack of it, will help in this respect

☑ We need to recognise that broad or vague questions will invite a variety of answers

☑ We praise correct answers; when correcting wrong answers we try to find something positive in them

In this chapter we have looked at two methods that could be used particularly in subjects that are more knowledge or theory-based, with an emphasis on how this might be achieved in a manner that encourages learning, as opposed to just delivering the required information. The principles apply to all subjects, however, as although in some specialisms the focus may be on the acquisition of skills or the influencing of attitudes, these are based on some form of knowledge or theory which will also have to be taught as part of the process.

The next chapter examines how acquired knowledge and theory can be used to develop practical skills.

Chapter summary

The main points covered in this chapter are:

✓ Whatever your subject it will involve the teaching of some theory

✓ The lecture can be effective in imparting theory to learners provided learner attention span and use of visual aids are considered

✓ Active learning methods can be combined with the lecture to maintain attention and help learners to process information

✓ Note-taking can be enhanced if it is structured

✓ Question and answer aids the acquisition of theory and provides feedback

✓ The purpose of the question will determine how it is shaped

✓ Direct questioning of individual learners can be conducted in a non-threatening manner by using the 'pose, pause, pounce, praise' sequence

✓ When responding to answers reinforce correct answers and try to find something positive in all of them

✓ Checklists for lecture and question and answer were provided

→ References

Brookfield, S.D. (2006) *The Skillful Teacher: On Technique, Trust, and Responsiveness in the Classroom*, (2nd Edn). San Francisco: Jossey-Bass.

Dale, E. (1969) *Audio Visual Methods in Teaching,* (3rd Edn). Orlando: Holt, Rinehart and Winston.

 Further reading

Bligh, D.A. (2000) *What's the Use of Lectures?* San Francisco: Jossey-Bass.
Although a bit 'academic' in its tone, this book covers all the aspects of the lecture as a teaching method you could possibly want to know about. Chapters 18 and 19 give some ideas for using combinations of methods to give a more active approach overall.

Brown, G. and Atkins, M.J. (1988) *Effective Teaching and Learning in Higher Education*. London: Routledge.
Chapter 3 has a particular focus on the skills of lecturing. Whilst aimed at lecturers in Higher Education, this does have broader application.

🖱 Useful websites

Active learning

www.geoffpetty.com/activelearning.html

www.teachtech.ilstu.edu/additional/tips/newActive.php

www.fctl.ucf.edu/teachingandlearningresources/selectedpedagogies/teachingmethods/content/activelearningguidelines.pdf

Mini whiteboards

www.educationworld.com/a_lesson/lesson/lesson251.shtml

How to teach skills

Chapter overview

When you have worked through this chapter on the teaching of skills you will be able to:

- Define a skill
- Identify the characteristics of skilled performance and potential effects on the teaching of skills
- Conduct a skills analysis
- Prepare for and conduct an effective demonstration
- Recognise the importance of monitoring and feedback for performance
- Prepare for and run effective skills practice sessions

Skills teaching

It may be that, although your learners need a certain amount of theory, the majority of your teaching involves them in acquiring skills. Skills can take many different forms; for example, social skills, key skills, intellectual skills. Whilst the content of this chapter could be applied to a greater or lesser extent to all of these, the focus will be on the teaching and acquisition of practical skills. Skills such as:

- Hairdressing – hair colouring
- Beauty – applying a face mask
- Bricklaying – laying two courses of bricks
- Catering – chopping an onion
- Motor vehicle – cleaning and setting a spark plug
- Engineering – setting up a lathe
- Electrical – testing a ring mains circuit

- Plumbing – bending pipes to a given angle
- Sport – performing a standing somersault
- Pottery – putting a handle on a mug
- Childcare – changing a nappy
- Art – applying a background wash

Do you teach such a skill? The list is endless, particularly in the lifelong learning sector with its emphasis on vocational courses, so do not be offended if we have missed you out!

Defining a skill

Before we look at the methods used in the teaching of practical skills it is worth first of all exploring the nature of a skill itself. What exactly do we mean by the term 'skill'? Write down your thoughts in the activity box.

Activity 7.1

A skill is:

One definition of skill is:

An organised pattern of mental and/or physical activity

This definition suggests that there is a 'knowledge' part to a skill and a 'doing' part, and such skills are generally referred to as 'psycho-motor'. The balance of these components varies in different skills. Riding a bicycle, for instance, will have a greater 'doing' component, whereas using a computer will have a greater 'knowledge' component, but **all** skills will have elements of each.

Another way of considering skills is to look at the characteristics of skilled performance. What makes it look as if someone is 'skilled' compared to another person? Can you think of an example where you have seen a skill performed well? What did you see that suggested to you that one performance could be considered as 'skilled' whereas another could not?

One characteristic which you may have spotted is the speed of completion of the job. Skilled performers will be quicker than those who are not. How many other characteristics can you think of? Record your answers in the next activity box.

Activity 7.2

A performance is skilled when:

How do your answers compare with the following?

Characteristics of the product

- High quality
- Fast output
- No wastage of materials

Characteristics of movements

- Economy of movement
- Ease, smoothness
- Continuity, confidence
- No hesitation
- Lack of fatigue

If you are involved in the teaching of skills you will yourself be a 'skilled performer' and so will exhibit the above characteristics. By the time we have become skilled, most of what we do has become automatic; we do not have to think about it. Because of this we may not even be aware of all of the actions that we make. When we teach skills, it is easy to forget all that is involved and make a number of assumptions, concerning the nature of the skill itself and the readiness of the learners. You can test this by asking someone, a friend or colleague, to write down the instructions for taking a match from a box and lighting it. Ask a different person to read the instructions and follow them to the letter!

Skills analysis

To overcome the making of assumptions, the first stage in teaching a skill is to break the skill down into its component parts so that we are aware of all that is involved and can pass this information on to our learners. This process is known as **skills analysis**.

In analysing a skill we are looking to answer questions such as:

- What are the specific actions involved in the skill?
- What is the exact sequence?
- What information is taken in through the senses at each stage?
- What decisions have to be made in the execution of the skill?
- What specific difficulties are associated with this particular skill?

In arriving at the answers to questions such as these, we first break the skill down into a number of smaller sub-skills. Each sub-skill is then broken down further until a level of detail appropriate to the existing knowledge and experience of learners is reached.

This is similar to the way in which the specifications for the competence-based approach of NVQs (National Vocational Qualifications) were devised. A skilled person was observed and through a process of task analysis the skill was broken down into units, elements and finally performance criteria.

In teaching bicycle riding, this could be similar to:

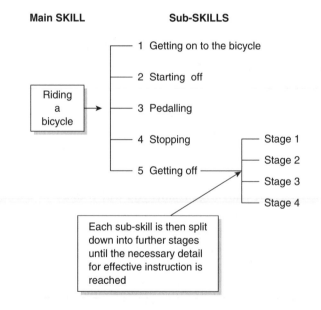

![Activity icon] **Activity 7.3**

Think of a skill that you currently teach or could teach. Conduct a skills analysis as shown above.

Now you recognise the need and know how to analyse a skill we can use the analysis to consider the best way to demonstrate the skill to our learners. Generally, we use **demonstration** to impart the 'knowledge' component of a skill and some kind of practical activity or **practice** session to consolidate this 'knowledge' and then acquire the 'doing' component. A typical skills session will contain both of these activities, the nature of the skill determining the relative amounts of each.

Demonstration

One of the most important factors to remember when giving a demonstration is that not only are you showing learners what to do in the performance of the particular skill, you are also showing them how to go about it. It is therefore essential to consider not only the content of the demonstration but also the attitudes which you display when carrying out the demonstration. These might be attitudes towards issues of safety, hygiene or standards of work. It is easy to fall into a 'do as I say, not as I do' frame of mind, but what learners should be exposed to is good practice incorporating correct attitudes.

In the next chapter we examine strategies to bring about change in attitudes. In skills teaching, however, it is better to teach appropriate attitudes to begin with and the most effective way of doing this is to model the attitude we would like to see our learners adopt.

Good demonstration exhibits the following positive features:
- ☑ It allows us to give a concrete example by showing practical application
- ☑ We can show how theory and practice link
- ☑ As demonstration is visual it is more easily understood and we can hold learners' attention more effectively
- ☑ We show correct practice – method, movement, pace

Activity 7.4

Think back to demonstrations you have seen:
What worked well?

What did not work very well?

What could have been done to make them better?

How to prepare for a demonstration

The secret of a good demonstration is the same as for most activities – good preparation and planning. This will involve:

Preparation of learners

- ☑ Making sure they know the purpose of the demonstration and any specific points on which to focus

Preparation of self

- ☑ Conducting a skills analysis to ensure clear guidance and a comprehensive commentary are given
- ☑ Deciding how much of the skill is to be demonstrated at one time and arriving at an overall strategy for carrying out the demonstration

Preparation of environment

- ☑ Making sure that everyone will be able to see and hear
- ☑ Considering whether the demonstration is best observed from the front or from behind
- ☑ Deciding whether to demonstrate to the whole group or whether to split them up into smaller groups and demonstrate to each group in turn

Preparation of materials and equipment

- ☑ Making sure you have sufficient of the correct material
- ☑ Ensuring all the equipment to be used is in good working order
- ☑ Arranging for technician support if required

How to conduct a demonstration

When we give a demonstration the sequence of 'whole, parts, whole' is often used. First the whole skill is demonstrated as a skilled performance. This attracts and focuses attention but also allows the learner to acquire a 'feel' for the complete skill and subsequently identify how the different parts of the skill fit together. There is a danger at this stage, however, that learners may be intimidated by a lengthy, perfect performance, leading to thoughts of 'I will never be able to do that!'. The complexity of the skill and previous experience and confidence of the learners should be considered when deciding how best to carry out the initial 'whole' demonstration.

The skill can then be broken into the sub-skills resulting from the skills analysis. Each of these is demonstrated, with explanation, at a pace that allows the learners to appreciate what it entails. The accompanying commentary or explanation will direct learners' attention to specific actions but may not focus exclusively on the 'how to do' parts of a skill but might also give reasons as to the 'why'. There may also be some highlighting of the use of the senses in the particular skill:

Sight   'if you watch for ...' 'at this stage you will probably see ...'
Hearing   'if you hear ... you will know that ...' 'you should listen carefully to ...'

Touch	'a light but firm grasp is needed ...' 'if you grasp it too tightly ...'
Taste	'... normally produces a taste like ...' 'if it tastes of ... you will know that ...'
Smell	'it should now smell like ...' 'note this particular smell. It means that ...'

Although in some skills the role of a particular sense is greater or less (for example, in cooking: taste and smell; pottery: touch; music: hearing and touch) all skills have some kind of sensory input, and drawing learner's attention to this gives a greater feel and understanding of the skill in question.

We can make the demonstration more participative and more of an 'active learning' experience at this stage by involving learners through the use of questioning. Questions can ask learners to **explain** – how can this be done?'; **predict** – 'what do you think comes next?'; **analyse** – 'why do you think I did that at this point?'; or **summarise** – 'what were the first three things I did in this demonstration?'.

Finally we would demonstrate the whole skill again at a competent pace reinforcing all that we have previously demonstrated.

Demonstration reminders

☑ Keep the demonstration short and simple; build up complex skills through a number of demonstrations if necessary

☑ Practise performing the skill slowly in order to emphasise the key points that should be highlighted in the commentary

☑ Make demonstrations more interactive by asking questions and by encouraging learners to predict what comes next

---

Effective practice

We need to consider three aspects in order to run effective skills practice sessions:

1 Preparation and starting off

After the demonstration, learners are in a position where they know what has to be done. This is not the same as being able to do it. The 'doing' part of the skill is acquired through practice and learners will need appropriate feedback on how they are performing in order to improve. Again, planning and preparation are essential if this activity is to run successfully. This will involve considering questions like:

Preparation of learners

What clothing is appropriate/required? Are learners fully aware of the various Health and Safety rules and requirements? Do they recognise that learning a skill may take time and progress may at times be slow?

Preparation of self

Have you established the criteria and stages involved in this skill? Do you know who are the learners more and less likely to take on the new skill quickly, more and less enthusiastic, more and less disciplined; have you a plan to cater for these factors?

Preparation of environment

Does everyone have sufficient working space and light? Are they able to move safely about the room? If not, how will you deal with this? Will you have to 'double up', and if so, how will you organise this? Does the staff:learner ratio fall within safety guidelines?

Preparation of materials and equipment

Are there sufficient materials and equipment of a suitable quality to meet the needs of the session? Do you need a handout or checklist along the lines of a skills analysis for learners to use?

Classroom management and the maintenance of an orderly environment are important in any kind of teaching that we undertake but in a practical situation this becomes an even more important consideration as inappropriate behaviour can lead to serious consequences. Practical classes need to be started off in a controlled and organised manner. This will involve gathering the group together in a convenient spot and addressing them as a whole. Clothing and equipment can be checked, health and safety considerations reinforced along with ground rules for this particular session. More practical matters such as time limits and procedures for the session – working singly or in pairs, expectations of progress, and use of tools, can then be covered before learners start work.

2 Monitoring

Our role during the practice session is that of monitoring individual progress and giving feedback, making sure learners know how they are getting on. One of the purposes of this is to ensure correct practice.

Whilst it is true that we can learn from mistakes, it is better to avoid them at this stage of acquiring a skill. Incorrect practice needs to be identified and corrected at the earliest opportunity before it becomes a habit. Once a learner has practised even a small part of a skill in an incorrect or inefficient manner, it can prove difficult for them to change their way of doing things to the desired method.

Initially then, monitoring involves ensuring that everyone is using the correct technique to carry out the skill and intervening when learners are having difficulty or are using incorrect methods. This may involve us in using 'on the spot' mini demonstrations, questioning or using the performance of other learners to guide individuals back onto the correct track.

When we have achieved this, monitoring becomes much more a case of checking progress and ensuring all learners remain engaged despite different rates of development. We need to give extra thought to those learners who acquire the skill more quickly to ensure that they remain involved and challenged. We can achieve this by suggesting different contexts or problem-solving scenarios to extend their use of the skill. Ways to develop further can be agreed with individual learners to encourage further improvement and to cater for the range of aptitudes within the group. Similarly, we need to consider the needs of those learners who find acquisition of the skill more difficult and therefore progress at a slower rate. Perhaps it will be necessary to set short-term goals or targets in such cases as part of the differentiation process.

3 Giving feedback

It is important to learners to know how they are doing whilst acquiring a skill so our feedback matters to them. How else do they know if their practice is correct or if they are making progress?

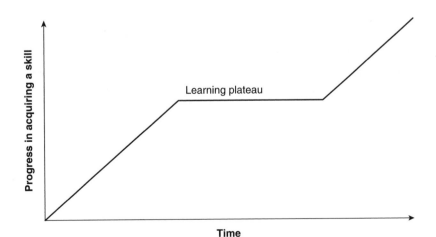

Activity 7.5

You have been learning a new skill. What kind of feedback do you want and how would you like it to be given?

Feedback, whatever its purpose, should be constructive. Good feedback acknowledges what the learner is doing correctly and identifies clearly and concisely what can be done to further improve performance. Good feedback also incorporates appropriate use of praise, particularly important for learners to whom the acquisition of the skill does not come that easily.

Motivation is extremely important in the process of skills acquisition, and when a learner has been progressing well it can be frustrating when improvement begins to slow down. This can frequently happen; learners can improve their performance rapidly to begin with but then tend to 'plateau' as the skill is consolidated. Learners often need to be helped through this time of apparently slow progress, illustrated in Figure 7.1.

Learning plateau

Progress in acquiring a skill

Time

Figure 7.1

Learner independence

Ultimately we want the learner to be able to perform the skill on their own without assistance or supervision – we want the learner to be independent of the teacher in their use of the skill. How quickly this is achieved can be influenced by two factors:

1 The amount of assistance given to learners
2 The way in which feedback is given

Giving assistance

If a learner is struggling with a particular aspect of a skill, there is a great temptation to help them over their immediate difficulty by giving step-by-step instruction or even by 'doing it for them' in an extreme case, on the basis that motivation will suffer if they cannot overcome this particular hurdle.

Whilst we want learners to remain motivated and not suffer from a potential stumbling block to their progress, we have to consider the extent to which the above remedies tend to encourage dependence on the teacher. The positive influence on learners' motivation of excessive help, no matter how well intentioned, is also debatable. It is hard to feel a sense of achievement knowing that someone else has done most of the work for you!

We need to find other ways around the problem, such as supplementary exercises that allow the learner to overcome a particular obstacle that is impeding progress by themselves, thus maintaining their control over their own learning.

Activity 7.6

Can you think of any other strategies for increasing learner independence when learning a practical skill?

One way in which we encourage learner dependence or independence is related to the way in which we give feedback to learners. There are essentially two styles that can be employed; either **telling**:

> That's good so far, although you might have … just try that and when you have finished, let me know and I'll come back and check it for you

or **asking**:

> That's interesting – why did you do it that way? Do you think it's the best way? Can you see a different approach? What do you think you need to do next?

Activity 7.7

What do you think are the advantages and limitations of each approach to giving feedback?

	Advantages	**Limitations**
Telling		
Asking		

'**Telling**' is quicker, to the point and gives confidence to learners, particularly if they have limited experience in using the particular skill. These are important considerations when you have a number of learners to attend to and a limited time in which to achieve this. Learners may still be unsure of themselves and their capabilities and appreciate straightforward advice and guidance. Potentially, however, when the teacher is no longer there to give advice and guidance, confidence disappears and so 'telling' can lead to dependence on the teacher.

'**Asking**', on the other hand, invites learners to self-evaluate progress and arrive at their own conclusions, thus making them much more independent. Learners may, however, see this approach as intimidating, particularly if they are limited in their ability to analyse and evaluate.

Which approach to use then? Some learners can cope with a more provocative or challenging method of questioning whereas others may require a more supportive approach. The answer is that we use whichever is the most appropriate in a given circumstance but as a general rule we should try to 'wean' learners away from reliance on the teacher and help them to become more independent in their learning and performance of the skill.

In this chapter we have looked at the acquisition of skills and how teachers might best go about facilitating this process. As well as acquiring the physical skill we will also want our learners to acquire appropriate attitudes towards the use of that skill. Attitudes towards standards for instance; will our learners want to use the skills they have acquired to do a 'proper job' or will they consider a 'good enough' job to be sufficient? Although we have taught them safe working practices, will they carry these out or take 'unsafe' shortcuts? The next chapter deals with attitudes and how we can influence them and although aimed primarily at those who teach subjects that are attitudinal in themselves, it contains much food for thought for those who teach practical skills.

Chapter summary

The main points covered in this chapter are:

- ✓ The definition and characteristics of a skill and skilled performance
- ✓ The first stage of teaching a skill is to conduct a skills analysis – break the skill down into its component parts
- ✓ Effective demonstration involves preparation of learners, self, environment and materials
- ✓ The commentary to a demonstration should be as interactive as possible and include reference to the sensory inputs involved in using the skill
- ✓ Learners acquire skills through structured practice sessions
- ✓ The teacher's role during practice sessions is to monitor learner progress and give constructive feedback
- ✓ Care must be taken not to encourage learner dependence on the teacher when acquiring a practical skill

→ Further reading

Hillier, Y. (2005) *Reflective Teaching in Further and Adult Education.* London: Continuum.
A useful demonstration checklist in Chapter 6 – A Practical Guide, 'Teaching and Learning Methods'.

Petty, G. (2004) *Teaching Today,* (3rd Edn). Cheltenham: Nelson Thornes.
Chapter 13 discusses different aspects of demonstration and Chapter 16 discusses issues related to supervising practical sessions.

Reece, I. and Walker, S. (2007) *Teacher Training and Learning: A Practical Guide,* (6th Edn). Sunderland: Business Education Publishers.
Chapter 1 includes a section which looks specifically at planning for the teaching of skills and gives a good example of skills analysis.

Useful websites

Examples of skills analysis

www.videojug.com/

How to teach subjects involving attitude change

Chapter overview

When you have worked through this chapter on teaching involving attitude change you will be able to:

■ Recognise the importance of attitudes in all areas of learning
■ Identify the components of an attitude
■ Describe how creating 'dissonance' within the components of an attitude can lead to attitude change
■ Identify methods you can use to promote attitude change
■ Recognise how you can use discussion to bring about attitude change
■ Use discussion effectively in a learning situation
■ Recognise how role play can be used to bring about attitude change
■ Describe how to run effective role plays

The importance of attitudes

In the previous two chapters we have focused on the knowledge and skills related to your subject specialism that you will want to pass on to your learners. Rather than focusing on knowledge or skills, some subjects are largely concerned with bringing about attitude change. Consider the following subject specialisms:

- **Skills for Life** – involves the acquisition of literacy and numeracy skills and knowledge but often the biggest barrier to success lies in negative attitudes towards the subject or towards self.
- **Counselling** – if students exhibit a judgemental attitude or lack of empathy towards others, no amount of knowledge or practice of skills will turn them into effective counsellors.

- **Customer Care** – requires knowledge of legislation related to customer transactions and the acquisition of skills and techniques to use in customer service, but a large part of learning concerns attitudes towards customers.
- **Nursing** – whilst medical knowledge and skills are of paramount importance, attitudes towards patients also play a large part in successful nursing.
- **Childcare** – it is difficult to see how learners could be successful in this field without a positive attitude towards children with whom they work.

Whatever your subject or skill you may nonetheless wish to develop certain attitudes in your learners. Consider what these might be by completing the next activity.

 Activity 8.1

I would like to bring about a change in the attitudes of my learners towards:

Perhaps you teach practical skills and would like to change learners' attitudes towards theory classes; if you teach plumbing or catering you may be concerned about attitudes to accuracy or careful presentation. You may teach Key Skills and have to overcome negative attitudes towards the subject itself. Maybe you work in a laboratory or workshop setting and need to address attitudes towards safety. Perhaps, in the groups you teach, bullying or making fun of others takes place and what you wish to address is learners' attitudes towards each other. Possibly it is learners' attitudes to standards of work that you wish to challenge or maybe even attitudes towards themselves. The list is fairly long and hopefully you agree that attitudes are important in all aspects of learning, irrespective of subject!

So, what are the appropriate methods of bringing about attitude change and how might we manage these most effectively? To help answer this question we need first to consider some theory.

Attitude formation and change

One useful approach to attitudes is the Structural Approach, which suggests that attitudes are made up of three separate but related parts:

1 **Beliefs:** We have some knowledge of whatever it is we hold an attitude towards, acquired either from our own experience or some other source. The knowledge that informs your attitude towards asylum seekers for instance may come either from being an asylum seeker, from having had contact with an asylum seeker, having read about asylum seekers in the newspapers or from having seen a programme on TV. This knowledge then may be first-hand or it may be second-hand, but whichever it is, it is open to interpretation. It is what we believe to be

the case based on our selection from the facts or experiences to which we have been exposed. For this reason it is called our belief.

2 **Feelings:** Suppose you have a strong, negative attitude towards drinking and driving. Upon hearing of a case where a drink-driver has caused a serious accident but you perceive the person has 'got away with' a fine in court rather than a prison sentence, you may well be filled with anger. This second component of an attitude concerns not what we believe we know about the subject of our attitude but how it makes us feel. Anything towards which we hold an attitude will evoke an emotional response or 'gut feeling'. The intensity of the feeling will depend upon how strongly we hold the attitude in question.

3 **Actions:** How would we know what attitude you hold towards dogs? If you were approached by a large, boisterous dog and you smiled and went to stroke it, we would know your attitude was positive. If, on the other hand, you looked uncomfortable or crossed the road to avoid the dog, it would be reasonable to assume your attitude was less than positive. Our actions – what we do (or do not do) – form the third component of an attitude.

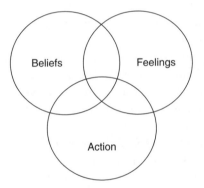

Together these three components make up the whole attitude. We can represent this as in the diagram above.

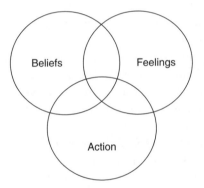

Activity 8.2

The table below contains three components of a positive attitude towards politics. Identify which is the belief (B), action (A) or feeling (F).

I get angry when I hear politicians being unjustly criticised	
I always vote at my local elections	
Everyone should be aware of the current political issues	

In Chapter 3 we looked at the concept of 'academic self-concept'. The self-concept we hold is an indicator of the attitude we have towards ourselves. If we take the example of a negative academic self-concept it gives rise to an attitude which, when broken down into its different components, looks like this:

BELIEF

The work that is given to me is too hard
and I cannot do it

FEELING

I get anxious every time I get given some work to do

ACTION

I try to avoid doing the work if I can

As we can see, although this is a negative attitude, all the components fit with each other in a coherent manner. The result is an individual who is unhappy and unsuccessful in their learning.

When all of the components of an attitude match or fit as in the above example, they are in a state of equilibrium and the attitude is said to be in a state of **consonance**. Happily not all attitudes are negative, of course, and a positive attitude can also result in balance between the three parts of the attitude and therefore be in a state of equilibrium.

Suppose, however, the learner in the above example now meets a teacher with whom they strike up rapport and the teacher takes the time to give simple clear explanations, set short-term achievable targets and give lots of positive feedback and praise. The result is a learner who feels capable of doing the work set and getting it right.

The components of the attitude the learner holds can no longer be said to be in equilibrium. There is a tension between them and the attitude is now said to be in a state of **dissonance**.

BELIEF

I am capable of doing the work and getting it right

FEELING

I get anxious every time I am given some work to do

ACTION

I try to avoid doing work if I can

A parallel can be drawn here with the human body, which works most effectively at a temperature of 98.6 degrees centigrade. If the body temperature drops below this, shivering occurs until the correct temperature, or equilibrium is reached again. Similarly, if body temperature becomes too high, perspiration brings it back into equilibrium. Physically, the body likes to maintain its 'status quo'. Similarly, the mind would like to maintain its state of equilibrium – it wishes to return to **consonance** as dissonance creates a feeling of tension.

How then can our learner return to a state of consonance? There are two options:

1 Focus on the belief that they cannot do the work:

> OK, it works with this one teacher but it's a 'flash in the pan'. It doesn't work with other teachers. Things haven't really changed at all and when this teacher leaves, things will be just as they were before.

The new positive belief is overridden by a negative belief and a state of agreement between the three components of the attitude has been regained. The tension of dissonance has now been relieved, but as a result the attitude has not been changed.

2 Perhaps, however, the new belief is so strong that it cannot be overridden. The learner still feels a psychological tension as the new belief clashes with existing feelings and actions. In this case, to achieve consonance feelings and actions must change to fall in line with the new belief:

BELIEF

I am capable of doing the work and getting it right

FEELING

I get a sense of satisfaction from being successful
and am becoming happy in my learning

ACTION

I put my energy into working hard

Now all of the components sit happily with each other and the psychological tensions due to dissonance have disappeared. In achieving this, the original negative attitude has changed to a positive attitude.

Bringing about change

What the theory outlined above tells us is that, if we can bring about a lasting change in one of the components of an attitude, the result could be an eventual change in the attitude as a whole.

It also tells us that we have three directions from which we can approach this task: changing beliefs, changing feelings or changing actions. An example of trying to achieve attitude change towards drinking and driving through affecting the action component can be seen in random breath testing. In an educational setting we might give penalties for handing in work late or some kind of reward for consistent punctuality. It could be argued, however, that compliance rather than attitude change is all that is being achieved.

In a teaching situation we would normally try to influence either beliefs or feelings. If we consider beliefs first, we could bring about change by altering the information base on which the beliefs are held, telling people what the appropriate beliefs are so they would also adopt them. Telling, however, only has a limited effect. We hold more strongly to a new belief when we arrive at it ourselves rather than being told by others and this is achieved by using active methods such as discussion.

Discussion

Discussion can be thought of as an activity where learners, or we and our learners, talk to each other with the intention of exchanging knowledge, ideas and opinions in order to arrive at some form of conclusion. Appropriate topics for groups to jointly explore in a discussion would be based around issues rather than facts as our purpose in using this approach is to raise awareness, solve problems, explore issues or make decisions. Some initial planning is required as the group needs to possess a certain level of knowledge on the discussion topic and the process has to be carefully managed to ensure the discussion maintains its focus.

As a learning activity, discussion has a number of positive features:

- Learners are encouraged to actively contribute to the session, share experience and learn from others
- Learners can explore ideas in a safe and secure setting, allowing them to gain clearer understanding and reconsider their views
- Learners can gain in self-confidence
- It gives us an indication of the level of understanding within the group
- It can be used to secure agreement within the group around given issues
- Learners have opportunities to exhibit their knowledge
- Learners can assimilate information together, which encourages the process of group formation

Equally, discussion can have a number of limitations. Most of these concern the participants themselves. Some prefer to be 'taught' and do not find it easy to participate in discussion. Some may try to dominate the discussion whilst others may opt out. Some may not take the activity seriously and others may miss the point altogether or deviate from the topic under discussion in their contributions. Most of these particular limitations can be overcome, however, by effective management of the group and of the discussion, as we shall see.

Activity 8.3

Think back to some past experience of discussion method where you may have learnt very little or even nothing at all. Jot down a few notes on why this was so and what could have been done to improve the situation.

Now do the same for an effective discussion – where you or group members learned a lot, were successful, enjoyed it and were interested. What was it that made it so good?

You will have identified a number of factors which lead to effective discussion but perhaps the most important of these relates to the atmosphere in which the discussion is carried out. This needs to be characterised by feelings of equality and trust; we need to establish ground rules relating to listening, interruptions and confidentiality.

In your reflections on ineffective discussions you may well have identified a lack of clarity over what was being discussed and a lack of shared purpose as being root causes. Often, however, the reason can be much simpler and lie in the arrangement of the furniture in the room. It is difficult to discuss, for instance, when the group are sitting in rows. Informality and all-round eye contact are essential for productive and inclusive discussion and this is normally achieved by placing chairs in circles, preferably without tables or any other physical barriers to communication.

Another possible danger is that of learners 'pooling ignorance' – perhaps making inappropriate comments or lines of argument or maybe reinforcing undesirable stereotypes. In this instance it might be wise to participate in or lead the discussion rather than let it proceed down an unproductive path. Although a discussion may be open-ended it will nonetheless have a purpose; some management or leading of the discussion may be necessary to make sure this is achieved.

In the case of attitude change, however, discussion is intended to challenge existing beliefs and ideas. In order for this to be achieved, these must be expressed in the first place. The process of querying and challenging needs to be carefully handled, as the beliefs that learners will hold most strongly arise out of their own experiences and are based on conclusions they themselves have reached. Existing beliefs are personal and challenges to these beliefs can be taken personally. An objective approach has to be taken, based on questioning and presentation of facts. Good leadership of discussion also involves summarising at frequent intervals, particularly at the end of the discussion. In the case of attitude change summaries should be prefaced by 'so what you are telling me' *or* 'what we seem to be agreeing on' to reinforce the notion that conclusions have come from the group and the process of discussion rather than from the teacher.

There are a number of strategies we can employ to make discussion more productive and more likely to serve its intended purpose:

Discussion is most effective when we have a clear agreed purpose in mind and a subject that lends itself to some form of deliberation

- ☑ Make sure the choice of topic is relevant and allows scope for discussion
- ☑ Ensure everyone is aware of the purpose of the discussion
- ☑ Consider supplying some 'trigger' materials such as a short video clip, case study or newspaper article to contextualise and give an initial focus

Discussion is most effective when everyone feels a part of the process and their contributions matter

- ☑ Set ground rules for the discussion
- ☑ Use verbal or non-verbal cues to encourage active listening and dispel competitiveness
- ☑ Use questions to direct and redirect and to encourage participation
- ☑ Acknowledge contributions
- ☑ Avoid expressing own views; try and act as 'neutral chairperson'

Discussion is more effective when some definite conclusions are drawn

- ☑ Control the pace of discussion allowing time for response and reflection
- ☑ If necessary, break up the discussion into smaller segments
- ☑ Keep discussion focused and limit digression
- ☑ Summarise throughout the discussion at appropriate points
- ☑ Help individuals or groups to identify what has been learned and how it might affect attitudes in the future

---

Types of discussion

So far, we have looked at large group discussions but discussion can be just as effective in bringing about attitude change if conducted in smaller groups which, at a later stage, pool their thoughts. Small groups make for more participation and can be used to look at different aspects of a wider issue. A couple of ways of organising small group discussion are outlined below.

Snowball

Learners consider an issue individually and jot down their thoughts. They then form pairs and compare notes, looking for similarities and differences. Pairs then combine to form groups of four and again notes are compared before the group as a whole arrives at a conclusion which they can report back in a plenary session.

The name snowball reflects the way the groups build in size, rather like a snowball rolling down a hill. This type of group activity is particularly useful when learners are still fairly new to each other as it starts off with an individual learner talking just to one other person, having had time to think about what they say, before contributing to the larger group.

Buzz group

Learners are divided into small groups and given a specific task to complete or an issue to consider in a fairly short time. The different groups may all work on the same task or issue, different aspects of the same task or issue, or separate but related tasks or issues. This can be a particularly productive activity if well managed, as is suggested by the name which refers to the productive buzz of conversation which takes place around the room.

Role play

If we turn now to bringing about attitude change by affecting the 'feelings' component of an attitude, one effective activity we can use is role-play. Role play involves a learner or learners imagining they are in another role and acting and behaving as another person might in a given situation. It allows experience of a situation or practice of a technique or skill in a safe environment, where mistakes can be made without fear and learned from.

Activity 8.4

List the various role plays you can think of using or might have experienced. What was the purpose of each?

Role play can have one of several functions, depending upon the context in which it is used:

- To demonstrate or model a given behaviour, for example a receptionist in a hotel greeting a guest
- To practise a skill, for example buying a train ticket in a language class
- To review and analyse our actions, for example in sports coaching
- To encourage creativity, for example acting out a fantasy in a drama class

- To explore the feelings aroused in a given situation, for example in diversity training
- To gain empathy, for example being blindfolded in order to gain empathy with learners who are visually impaired

It is role play used with the last two kinds of intention that we will be focusing on in this chapter. We will be asking learners to 'walk in the other person's moccasins' as the Red Indians would say, in order to experience what others have felt. We hope that in doing this we will have an effect on the 'feelings' component of an existing attitude with the intention of introducing an element of 'dissonance' and thus begin the process of attitude change.

It is important to note at this stage that in this type of role play you will not be dealing with the logic and certainty of knowledge or facts, but with emotions that can sometimes be quite intense. Reactions can be unpredictable and managing this kind of activity requires its own particular skills and sensitivity. If you are new to role play it is a good idea to observe another teacher running one before trying it out yourself. It is not an activity to be used lightly and needs careful planning, which can be considered under the following headings.

Initial planning

As with all learning activities, you should give careful thought not only to identifying exactly what it is that the role play is to achieve but also to the characteristics of the group and individuals within the group with whom you intend to use the activity.

Considering the **exact purpose** of the role play will help you to make decisions about devising the role play itself and how best to manage the feedback session at the end of the exercise. The purpose will shape your answers to questions like:

- What kind of scenario will provide the desired experience but still be considered realistic? How many roles will be involved?
- How much time needs to be allocated to acting out the role play and how much for the feedback at the end?
- How should feedback be structured? Who should speak first – role players, others in the group, teacher?
- Should roles be allocated or should they be voluntary? Do role players need to be briefed before the session? Should the briefing take place by talking to participants or by giving them role cards or both?

Considering the **nature of the group** will help to decide how to run the activity and will answer questions like:

- Is the group sufficiently mature and confident to benefit from this type of activity? Have they used role play before? If so, how did it go and what can be learned from the previous experience?

- Are there particularly sensitive learners in this group I may have to watch out for?
- Are there particular learners that for some good reason I do or do not want to take on roles or to work together?
- Will the group benefit more from conducting the role play all together in one large group or splitting up into smaller groups?

Running the role play

We can now consider the practicalities, one of which is how to introduce the activity. Not all learners find role play to be a comfortable experience and so there can be resistance to the notion of role play. It may, therefore, be necessary to think of a non-threatening method of presenting the session to the group. This can be as straightforward as not using the term 'role play' but simply giving an overview of the activity and its purpose.

The next stage is to give an overview of the chosen scenario before briefing anyone to whom a role has been allocated. How this is done will depend upon the situation but often some form of written instruction works well. Participants will probably require a little time to prepare themselves and small groups can be used to help in this. At this stage it may be worth briefing the rest of the group, as although they may not be directly involved, they nonetheless have an important part to play. Perhaps there are particular issues or factors they can be alerted to or specific responses you particularly would like them to look out for.

Once everyone is ready, the activity can commence within previously set time limits.

The debrief

Arguably, this is the most important part of the activity. Role play is an example of an experiential approach and learning only occurs when the experience is reflected on and analysed. A well managed debrief is crucial if learning, and therefore attitude change, is to occur.

At its conclusion, you need to formally end the role play as a signal to the participants to step out of role and return to being 'their normal selves'. When this has been achieved and the attention of the group as a whole has been captured, a structured discussion can begin. One way of achieving this is to consider:

- What actually happened – what did observers see, what did role players feel?
- Some analysis – why do we think ..., how did that ...?
- What has been learned – what has been gained from the experience, what has been discovered, what are the implications?

Finally, learners need to take what has been learned and formally or informally arrive at some kind of action plan relating to the attitudes they will display in the future.

Case study

Consider the following case study:

The issue

You are a teacher of Engineering in a typical FE college. You teach HND Engineering and you are having a problem with one particular group who you have for workshop sessions. They are generally a hard-working and responsive group but they seem to have adopted some bad habits as a result of their work experience. The wearing of safety boots is a workshop rule that is being constantly ignored. When you try to address this issue with the group, you are met with comments like, 'Why should we have to wear boots here, they don't do it in the real world' and 'We're old enough to make our own decisions and it's our risk, isn't it?' It has now reached the stage where some kind of action must be taken, not least because of the impending visit by the course External Verifier.

How would you bring about a responsible attitude to working safely in general and wearing safety boots in particular with this group?

Write down your solution before reading on

Possible solutions

Affecting actions

- No admittance to the session without the appropriate footwear
- Admittance but have to sit to one side and watch as others carry out practical work
- Rent learner a pair of boots for the duration of the lesson
- Contact parents or employer, alerting them to the lack of appropriate footwear and your concerns for safety

Affecting feelings

- Videos of accidents and the ensuing injuries
- Role-play having to tell parents of injuries suffered by their offspring
- Role-play having to complete different tasks with one leg tied up

Affecting beliefs

- Presenting statistics on accidents
- Get them to write two lists – one on the reasons for wearing safety boots, one on the reasons for not wearing them; get them to compare the lists and justify not wearing boots.

Case studies can be a useful resource in changing attitudes by promoting and focusing discussion. They are not, however, particularly easy to write. Case studies should present an open issue but be based on clear objectives – what do you intend learners to learn as a result of using the case study? Content needs to be relevant, realistic and factually accurate whilst limiting itself to providing the essential background. Stereotypes should be avoided and inclusive images encouraged. Once you have selected a case study you then need to formulate questions that relate directly to your objectives.

Attitude change is not an instantaneous process – it has to be worked at over a period of time. Of the approaches suggested above, discussion is the more widely used and is certainly the more advisable approach if you are fairly new to teaching. Role play is a powerful method but can be unpredictable and difficult to manage.

Having looked at the different types of methods and activities that we can use within our different subject specialisms, the next chapter turns our attention to a consideration of the various ways we can support these through effective use of resources.

Chapter summary

The main points covered in this chapter are:

- ✓ All subject specialisms, either directly or indirectly, involve attitude change
- ✓ Attitudes are considered to consist of the three different but related components of beliefs, feelings and actions
- ✓ Normally, these three components are in balance, leading to a state of 'consonance' or psychological well-being
- ✓ Causing an imbalance or 'dissonance' between the three components can lead to attitude change
- ✓ Affecting actions can result in compliance rather than attitude change
- ✓ Discussion is used to bring about change in beliefs
- ✓ Discussion can be conducted as either a large group or small group activity
- ✓ Role play is used to examine feelings

→ Further reading

Most social psychology text books will contain a section on attitudes. A good example is:
Hayes, N. (1993) *Principles of Social Psychology*. Hove: Lawrence Erlbaum Associates.
Chapter 5 gives a reasonably in-depth but readable coverage, defining attitudes and examining change and measurement.
The classic text on role play is:
Van Ments, M. (1999) *The Effective Use of Role Play*, (2nd Edn). London: Kogan Page.

Useful websites

Dissonance and attitude change

www.afirstlook.com/archive/cogdiss.cfm

http://changingminds.org/explanations/theories/cognitive_dissonance.htm

9

Resources

Chapter overview

When you have worked through this chapter on resources you will be able to:

- Recognise the ways in which resources support the learning process
- Identify the range of resources at your disposal
- Describe how to make the most effective use of these resources
- Recognise some basic design principles that apply to all resources
- Reflect upon your current use of resources

How resources support learning

Learning takes place as a result of connections being made in the brain. We cannot control this; it happens automatically. We do have some say, however, in how the information reaches the brain in the first place. Information is sent and received in a number of ways that use our various senses – through our eyes (sight), our ears (hearing) and through our other senses such as touch, taste and smell.

The range of resources

If the use of resources promotes learning, we need to be aware of the resources we have at our disposal.

 Activity 9.1

List all of the resources you could use in the teaching of your subject

You will have come up with a number of possibilities. For simplification, we can divide these into four categories:

1 Prepared visual and aural material, possibly using slide projector, video, CD player, tape or cassette recorder, computer packages, Internet
2 Prepared written or diagrammatic material: textbook, handout, worksheet, charts, posters
3 Spontaneous recording on a whiteboard, flip chart, overhead projector
4 Models or the 'real thing'

You may find that most of your examples fall into one particular category depending on the type of teaching that you do, but you should be able to draw to a certain extent on all categories.

Using visual and aural material

In this first category we have a number of devices that allow us to use prepared resources. We can show slides or videos we have made ourselves, or which may have been commercially produced, to illustrate a wide range of topics. Specific software packages often on CD may be available for the computer. Computers can be linked to projection facilities. All of these are meant primarily for use with groups but can be used with individuals.

The list above contains a range of possibilities; you will doubtless have experienced a number of them.

 Activity 9.2

Outline how you could use at least one new resource in this category. Identify a specific session in which you could do this.

Using written and diagrammatic material

The second category consists of prepared written or diagrammatic resources. Charts and posters on the wall liven up a teaching room and can be referred to specifically during a session. Handouts provide a useful summary of content. Worksheets can be used to guide learners systematically through a process. Textbooks can provide a useful reference during a session as long as they are used to supplement, not guide, the teaching that is taking place.

Activity 9.3

How could you extend the range of resources you use in this category?

The proportion of information taken in by the senses will depend to some extent upon the nature of the activity in which we are engaged. Taste and smell, for instance, assume greater importance when cooking and a potter working on a wheel would place a greater reliance on touch. Generally, however, we take in most information by sight. Research shows that the split is approximately:

> 80% through our eyes
> 15% through our ears
> 5% through our other senses

The reception of information can be affected by a number of factors:

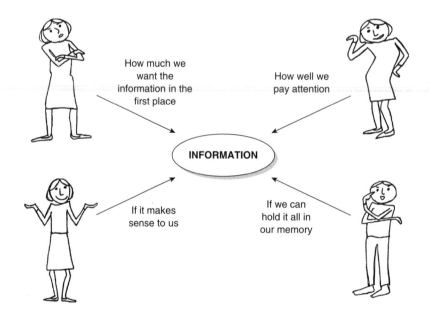

It is these factors that we can influence, and through effective use of resources we can:

Create interest: We add another dimension when senses other than hearing are brought into play. To be able to hear, see, touch and, maybe, even smell or taste what is being talked about brings the subject alive.

Attract and maintain attention: Visual resources, in particular, grab our attention. If you look back at the previous page of this book your eye will be drawn immediately to the diagram rather than any other part of the page. Visual material can provide a point of focus around which to structure information and highlight the most important points to be made.

Help understanding The more senses we can bring to bear, the more clues we have to help us to interpret the object or information under examination.

Make it easier to remember

Generally we remember best if:

- We are interested in the information
- We focus attention fully on it
- We can understand it

Resources help in all of these respects. There is a saying 'a picture paints a thousand words'. Visual resources act as pictures, reducing the bulk of information to be taken in.

Using resources spontaneously

The third category is concerned with resources we would use when recording or illustrating thoughts as we progress through a teaching session. They are more spontaneous in their use and we would generally write on them by hand, although there can be some preparation beforehand. The whiteboard, electronic whiteboard, flip chart and, occasionally, the overhead projector (OHP) are most useful for jotting down themes, ideas and examples.

Activity 9.4

What new use can you make of such resources?

Using models or the 'real thing'

All of the above, however, are substitutes for our fourth category, the 'real thing'. We cannot always introduce real items into the teaching environment. Introducing a plumbing system, a real body to resuscitate, a heart or the latest machine may be impracticable for reasons such as size, safety, availability or cost;

this is where we turn to other resources as a substitute. When it is possible to use the 'real thing' or alternatively a model, the impact is greater because the world we are learning about has been introduced into the session. The impact is even greater if the item can be touched and handled.

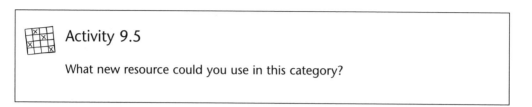

Activity 9.5

What new resource could you use in this category?

So, there is a variety of options available to us. Appropriate use of these will give our teaching interest and variety.

Designing resources for impact and purpose

To make the most of the resources you have selected, you will need to think about the best design and the most effective ways to use them. Some simple rules that apply to the use of all types of resource are:

- Resources should be used both appropriately and sparingly. They are intended to support, not lead learning. The intention is to enhance the message we are putting across, not distract from it.
- Ensure the resources you use reflect the diversity and experience of learners.
- Always check equipment is working before using it and you know how to operate it properly. Have a standby in case of equipment failure.

The majority of the resources we use are visual in nature. Whenever a visual aid is used, its function is to help the learner process information. We want to draw attention to the important points and organise them in such a way that makes it easier for learners to commit them to memory. We need to bear these points in mind whether we record information spontaneously, as with the whiteboard, electronic board or flip chart, or prepare it in advance, as with overhead projector transparencies or PowerPoint presentations.

Some of the more useful visual design techniques are illustrated in Figure 9.1. Generally, when considering any type of visual aid, we should:

- Use lots of space – avoid cluttering the visual with too much information
- Use colours to emphasise key points
- Remember lower case is easier to read than UPPER CASE
- Make sure all words and illustrations are large enough to be seen by everyone in the room

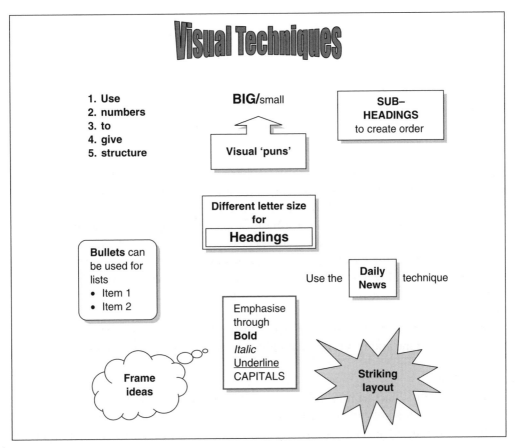

Figure 9.1

Effective use of resources

We turn now to making best use of the resources we have at our disposal. Information and Communication Technology (ICT) is playing an increasingly important role both as a resource itself, and in the production of the more traditional visual aids. Word processing and the storing and importing of different types of images allow the production of better quality and more effective visual aids, such as handouts and overhead transparencies, giving a more professional finish and appearance.

The advent of computerised projection systems means we can access the Internet on an individual or group basis and other possibilities are opened up as more multimedia software packages are developed and IT facilities become more widely available in the classroom. As yet, however, access to such technologies within many teaching environments is still fairly limited, and so we will be concentrating first on the more commonly available resources and visual aids before examining the possibilities that are opened up to us by electronic means.

1 Whiteboard

The whiteboard is a modern, cleaner, easier to use version of the old school chalkboard and fulfils much the same purpose. We would normally use whiteboards during teaching to:

- Record the main points or headings of the material we are covering
- Illustrate and clarify more complex or technical points
- Record responses and contributions from learners

We can prepare work in advance on a whiteboard, but flip charts or overhead transparencies are more suitable for this purpose. Even if the whiteboard is used in a spontaneous manner, we would normally have some idea in advance as to how we are going to display the information; will we group certain contributions together, use colours to highlight, bullets to add emphasis or headings to provide structure?

Whatever our decisions, our writing on a board needs to be tidy and large enough to be seen from all parts of the room. Achieving this, however, usually requires practice, as there is a tendency for writing to tail off across the board. It can be useful to mentally divide the board into two or three vertical segments and use these one at a time. When we have finished using the whiteboard, we should clean it, otherwise it may distract learners from what we are moving on to next. This does mean that we have no permanent record of what has been done and this is the main disadvantage of using the whiteboard.

2 Flip chart

We can use a flip chart to fulfil all the same functions as a whiteboard, although the flip chart is considerably smaller and will therefore hold less information at one time.

The additional advantage of the flip chart, as we mentioned earlier, is that we can use it to prepare information and diagrams in advance. Such prepared material, however, can act as a distraction if learners can see it before it is required. To maximise impact and avoid distraction we can use a blank sheet between prepared pages, giving the same effect as cleaning the whiteboard.

If we do not wish to display all of the information at one time, we can attach a blank flip chart sheet to the top of the page containing the information. We are then able to display the information gradually as and when appropriate. This is the equivalent of using the 'reveal' technique on the overhead projector, which we shall be considering next.

The flip chart has additional potential as a teaching resource as we can detach individual sheets from it and groups of learners can use these to work on. The results can be displayed on the walls, allowing further discussion of the points they contain.

A variation on this theme is when flip chart sheets with headings are placed around the teaching room and learners circulate, recording comments and ideas. This can then be used as the basis for group discussion.

3 Overhead projector

The overhead projector (OHP) is, quite simply, a machine that projects images onto a screen from a transparent film placed on top of it. It is largely being superseded by other more modern projection systems but a lot of the principles behind its use apply also to all of these newer systems. Our purpose in using the OHP is often to **highlight the main points**, so about six lines of text on a transparency is sufficient. We can gain the maximum effect from our transparencies by using the techniques of reveal, blocks and overlays.

Reveal

If we present all of the information on a transparency to learners at the same time, it can prove to be a distraction. On a list, for example, while we are explaining the first item, our learners' attention may be focused on reading and wondering about the subsequent items. Using the **reveal** technique allows us to control the rate at which information is presented by simply placing a piece of paper, or preferably card, over the top of the transparency and pulling it down gradually to 'reveal' information at the appropriate moment (Figure 9.2).

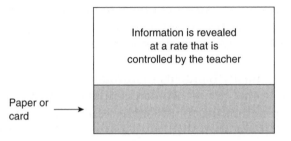

Figure 9.2

We can also present information selectively by the use of 'blocks', which cover bits of information on the transparency until it is required, thus allowing us to present the information a bit at a time in the sequence of our choice.

Overlays

Sometimes the information we wish to present is too complex to be presented all at once. If this is the case, we can break it down into smaller, more easily understood chunks, each on a separate transparency. We then build up the information or picture by laying the transparencies on top of each other. To make sure the images line up correctly, we can attach different transparencies around one that is central, making hinges with masking tape. The transparencies can then be folded over on top of the one at the centre, in the correct order, building up the information (Figure 9.3).

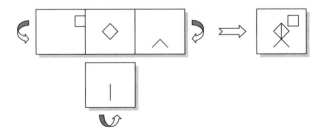

Figure 9.3

Controlling the rate at which information is presented by the methods outlined above allows us to have maximum impact on learning.

4 Handouts

During any teaching session, learners will often want to try to remember as much as possible of the information given. They cannot commit everything to memory and so will take notes whilst we are talking to them or copy information from the whiteboard, flip chart or whatever visual aid we happen to be using. This creates problems with attention, which is now divided between two different sources, as we noted in Chapter 6.

As we are aware of this, we might give out handouts that provide an accurate record of the session; these can be taken away, therefore freeing learners from the need to take copious notes. We do not have to provide an exact transcript of the session and may even simply copy the slides we are using. These are known as **summary** handouts and we normally give them out at the end of the teaching session.

We can also use summary handouts to introduce topics and refer to them as the session progresses. In this case we would distribute them at the beginning of or at some appropriate point during the teaching session. Unfortunately, these are the type of handout that are often filed away and never referred to again, or are left behind in the teaching room.

An alternative approach is to use the **incomplete** or gapped handout that has blank spaces for learners to fill in. This has the advantage that it allows a structured set of notes to be taken away, but it also involves the learner in an active consideration of the information included rather than merely passively recording it. In this way we can make the handout part of the teaching session rather than an extra and it is more likely to be referred to later. It provides a memory aid, not just for the information it contains, but also for the teaching session as a whole.

As well as for recording information, we can use incomplete handouts to:

- Test initial knowledge levels
- Promote discussion
- Test understanding in the session
- Encourage learners to arrive at solutions to problems
- Review previous experiences related to the current session
- Apply what has been learned
- Provide structure to group work

Presentation of handouts, as with other resources, can greatly enhance effectiveness. Images from the Internet can be used to increase visual impact and tables help in presenting information in an organised and more easily understood manner. To make best use of handouts, refer to the 'handout' in Figure 9.4.

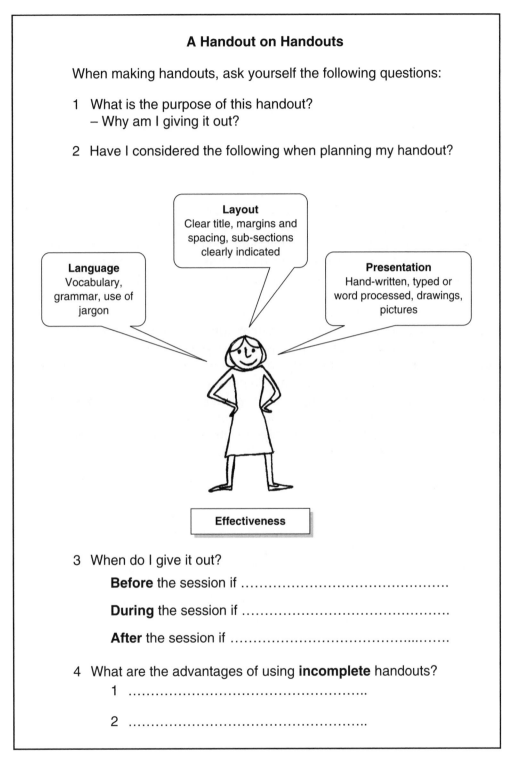

A Handout on Handouts

When making handouts, ask yourself the following questions:

1 What is the purpose of this handout?
– Why am I giving it out?

2 Have I considered the following when planning my handout?

Layout
Clear title, margins and spacing, sub-sections clearly indicated

Language
Vocabulary, grammar, use of jargon

Presentation
Hand-written, typed or word processed, drawings, pictures

Effectiveness

3 When do I give it out?

Before the session if ....

During the session if ....

After the session if ....

4 What are the advantages of using **incomplete** handouts?

1 ....

2 ....

Figure 9.4

5 The 'real thing' and models

The 'real thing', whether it be a particular tool, a specific item of equipment or even something as basic as part of an engine, is the ideal as it brings the real world into the teaching room. It can be passed round, touched, examined and invariably generates the kind of interest and discussion that other visual aids do not. As we noted earlier, we cannot always use the 'real thing' – it may be impracticable for reasons such as size, safety, availability and cost – and this is when we turn to other visual aids as a substitute.

6 PowerPoint presentations

PowerPoint is part of the Microsoft Office suite and is a program that allows you to create presentations with text, graphics, hyperlinks and sounds, displayed on a sequence of individual slides. Once the basic techniques of slide production have been mastered, it can be used to generate presentations quite quickly and easily. These are easily stored and modified electronically and by going to the 'print' mode, handouts, in a variety of formats, 'speaker's notes' and outlines can be printed as well as copies of the original slides.

PowerPoint has its origins in industry, where presentations were made in the boardroom. Its purpose was to present the greatest amount of information in the shortest time to a specific and knowledgeable group. So, care has to be taken in adapting what is primarily a 'business system' into a learning environment; it has to be used in a different manner as its purpose is to **support** learning and learning activities rather than **lead** a presentation. 'Death by PowerPoint' is now acknowledged as a major cause of fatalities in the learning environment.

We have already seen that the purpose of a visual aid is to attract and maintain attention, help understanding and make it easier to commit material to memory. Slides should therefore be simple and uncluttered and used to introduce, highlight or summarise rather than deliver large amounts of information. They should contain headings, short bulleted lists and visuals.

The same techniques as suggested for the overhead projector should be used with PowerPoint.

- Reveal and build effects can be achieved through Custom animation, which can be used to make text and pictures enter, exit or move
- The presentation can be left when it has served its immediate purpose and returned to when required by use of either the 'b' key on the keyboard (blanks out the screen and returns to the slide when pressed again) or the 'w' key (similar to 'b' key but turns the screen white)

Other useful controls are:

Key	Function
n	next part of slide
p	returns to previous image
number key and 'enter'	takes you to that number slide in the presentation
'ctrl' plus 'a'	displays a pointer (normally an arrow)
'ctrl' plus 'h'	hides the pointer
'ctrl' plus 'p'	changes the arrow to a pen.

Using hyperlinks, PowerPoint can be used to devise stand-alone learning packages which can be incorporated into Virtual Learning Environments (VLEs) (see below in this chapter).

PowerPoint, then, is a powerful resource but we need to remind ourselves that it is a visual **aid**. As such, it should complement rather than lead or dominate what we do if we wish to use it to best effect to aid learning.

7 The interactive whiteboard

An interactive whiteboard looks like, and can be used in the same way as, an ordinary whiteboard but has the added advantage that it connects to a computer and projector, allowing the computer's desktop to be displayed on the board's surface. The computer can be controlled from the board, as the pen acts like a mouse. This means that not only can the Internet, PowerPoint, or any other application that can be accessed by computer be displayed on the whiteboard, but anything which is recorded onto the whiteboard can be transferred to the computer and thus saved and retrieved for future use. This means that users, whether teacher or learner, can input both at the computer and at the board.

Different makes of whiteboard vary in their method of operation and come with different software and resources. The two major suppliers in the UK are Promethean and Smartboard, and it is worth visiting their websites (see end of chapter for addresses) as both contain user forums and offer free resources. Resources are mainly school-based, as under the government's 'Harnessing Technology' policy most schools in the country have interactive whiteboards in place, but resources may well be adaptable for other groups. What is significant here is that future lifelong learners will no doubt expect this technology as a norm!

Some of the common tools used include:

- Reveal blind (like holding a piece of paper over the OHP): The tool will go up/down/left/right. It can be used for columns as well as for lists
- Spotlight: Reveals only a section of the content on the board. Its shape and size can be varied and it can be moved around the board. This allows attention to be focused on specific items
- Timer: A digital or analogue clock which can either count down or count up and sits in the corner of the board; good for allowing groups to self-regulate the timing of group work
- Camera capture: Allow parts of text or images from any displayable source to be captured and placed on a new clean page for further discussion and annotation. This is especially useful when preparing lessons (copyright allowing)

It is important to remember that the whiteboard is interactive and not just a medium through which to route PowerPoint presentations – teachers and learners can use it either individually or collaboratively. To make the whiteboards even more interactive, classroom response systems are now being linked to them, allowing for comprehensive, instant feedback from learners. The idea of the response system is that each learner has a hand-held device like a remote control or small mobile phone. In its simplest mode this offers an A to F choice, so, as simple multi-choice questions come up on the interactive whiteboard, the group can respond. The responses are recorded by the whiteboard and can be viewed (probably at a later date) either as a pie chart (anonymously) or by learner's name.

Results can also be exported to Excel for future analysis and if required fed into a college's data management system for record keeping. As well as allowing responses to prepared material, the system can also be used spontaneously. At any point in the session questions can be written to the whiteboard and responses gained instantly.

Initial assessment of learners' levels of understanding can take place simply at the beginning of each session. Formative assessment can be carried out quickly and easily (see Chapter 10). It is relatively simple to give a 10 minute input then pose a few questions to help gauge whether learners have absorbed key points.

Opinions can be sought through questions such as 'Do you agree or disagree with the congestion charge?' Those who strongly agree can input 'A' and those who disagree input 'F'; those who have less strong opinions can choose somewhere in-between. It then might be interesting to take a poll again at the end the discussion/ debate to see if opinions have shifted. The initial responses can also be used to sit people of opposing views within smaller discussion groups. A further advantage is the possibility of giving anonymous answers. So if a 16 year old wants to respond that smoking is 'bad' they can see the response as part of an anonymous pie chart.

8 The Virtual Learning Environment (VLE)

A VLE is an application which allows learners to access, by computer, a variety of course-related learning materials and interactive systems contained within a dedicated website. Typically, a commercial VLE such as Blackboard will have different access rights for teachers and learners, teachers having editing rights with learners restricted to viewing rights.

On entering the VLE, a learner will usually encounter an announcement board with messages and course updates, and a series of navigation buttons which give access to the different materials contained within the VLE. These might include:

* Teaching materials such as course content and the resources used in taught sessions
* Administrative information and contacts
* Additional resources such as reading materials and web links
* Links to internal sources such as the library
* E-mail with other learners or groups of learners
* Discussion boards and chat rooms
* Learning packages, some of which might be interactive in nature
* Assessment activities, which may or may not be automatically marked

Whilst originally created for distance education, now the more common function of the VLE is to supplement taught sessions, complementing face-to-face contact with electronic contact as part of a 'Blended Learning' approach. This can be achieved by either providing 'trigger' materials and exercises in advance of a taught session or later follow-up exercises. Some short information-based parts of the course can be delivered through the VLE by taking learners through a structured sequence of materials that might include notes, PowerPoint presentations, videos, web links, short exercises and quizzes. As with most approaches using ICT, the challenge is to make the medium interactive rather than use it to deliver information in a passive manner.

In this chapter we have looked at a number of different resources and have perhaps inspired you to make use of a wider range of those available, or maybe even encouraged you to make greater use of those based on ICT. Whatever your thoughts, it is important to remember that the two important factors in getting the most out of your resources lie in:

1 The design of resources for impact and purpose
2 Making best use of resources

Evaluating resources

You are hopefully now more confident in both of these areas, but as in all aspects of teaching, use and reflection on that use provides the route to improvement. The checklist below will help you in that reflective process.

Checklist for using resources

1 *The resource*

☑ Did it achieve its purpose?
(create interest, affect attention, help understanding, aid memory)
☑ Did it use appropriate language levels for this group?
☑ Did it use inclusive images and examples?
☑ Was it 'uncluttered' and did it highlight the important learning points?
☑ Was it visually appealing?
☑ Did it give a good return for the effort spent in creating it?

2 *Use of the resource*

☑ Did I use it at the most appropriate time?
☑ Did I use it to engage learners and encourage active learning?
☑ Did I make sure it did not become a distraction?
☑ Did I make sure learners were aware of how to use it and what its purpose was?

Feel free to add to the checklist as you look at this on your PTLLS course.

Chapter summary

The main points covered in this chapter are:

✓ Resources help in the processing of information by creating interest, attracting and maintaining attention, helping understanding and aiding memory
✓ Resources fall into a number of different categories ranging from prepared resources to those which are used in a more spontaneous manner
✓ A consideration of principles of design helps to give maximum impact to visual resources
✓ Whiteboards and flip charts can be used to record spontaneous contributions as well as accommodating pre-prepared materials
✓ Overhead projectors are gradually being replaced by electronic systems such as interactive whiteboards and PowerPoint presentations but techniques such as gradual revealing or building up of material still apply
✓ The design of handouts is influenced by purpose but generally the use of 'gapped' handouts leads to a more active learning process
✓ Virtual Learning Environments are now being more commonly used to complement existing forms of delivery

Further reading

Petty, G. (2004) *Teaching Today – A Practical Guide*, (3rd Edn). Cheltenham: Nelson Thornes.
A highly readable book in which Chapter 35 'Resources for Teaching and Learning' gives a comprehensive coverage of the various resources used by teachers and Chapter 36 focuses specifically upon 'Learning with Computers'.

Hillier, Y. (2005) *Reflective Teaching in Further Education*, (2nd Edn). London: Continuum.
Chapter 5 'Developing Learning Resources' covers every resource imaginable with lots of good advice on both design and use.

Useful websites

http://feandskills.becta.org.uk

www.jisc.ac.uk/

www.intute.ac.uk/

www.e-learningcentre.co.uk/eclipse/Resources/whiteboards.htm

Promethean
  www.prometheanworld.com/index.php

Smartboard
  http://smarttech.com/

10

Assessing learning

Chapter overview

When you have worked through this chapter on assessing learning you will be able to:

- Identify the purposes of assessment
- Select assessment methods that are suited to the learning objectives and/or competences to be assessed
- Select assessment methods that are suited to where the learning is being assessed
- Define and recognise the importance of validity and reliability of assessment results
- Prepare learners to succeed in assessment
- Encourage learners to feel relaxed, ask questions and express their views
- Make an assessment decision and give constructive feedback to learners
- Complete assessment records, pass them to a relevant authority and store them securely

So far we have looked at ways of making teaching more effective; we have considered our learners, the setting of objectives, the methods that might be employed to enable learners to achieve these and the resources that might be used to support our chosen methods. If we look back to the planning cycle in Chapter 4, the other area we still need to think about is how we are going to check that the learners have achieved the learning objectives for the session.

We need now to consider the process of assessment and the methods we might use. Assessment quite simply means checking that learning has taken place. Thinking back to the journey analogy, we want to know whether we have arrived at the chosen destination.

Assessment can be defined more specifically

as all those activities and processes involved in judging performance or measuring learner achievement.

When we start to think further about assessment, there are a number of important questions it is useful to answer.

- **Why do we assess?**
  What is the purpose of the assessments?
- **What do we assess?**
  What are the assessments actually measuring?
- **How do we assess?**
  Why is this the most appropriate method to use?
- **When do we assess?**
  At what point in the course/session do these assessments occur?
- **Who assesses?**
  Are you the only person involved in the setting of the assessment and the decisions on the outcomes?
- **Where do we assess?**
  Does the assessment take place in the teaching environment or 'real life'?

Assessment methods

As we progress through this chapter, we will be dealing with each of the above questions in turn. First though, it will be helpful to identify the various methods that might be used. As a starting point, think about all the ways you know that can be used to check that learning has occurred and list these in the next activity box.

 Activity 10.1

My list of assessment methods:

We can ask learners to:

☑ Respond to questions

☑ Complete an exercise or test (short answer or multiple choice) either written or online

☑ Perform a task or skill whilst you observe

☑ Present evidence produced in the workplace

☑ Complete a project or assignment

☑ Write an essay

☑ Demonstrate to the rest of the group

☑ Discuss a real example

☑ Complete a piece of work to apply what they have learned and then report back to the rest of the group

☑ Take part in an aural or oral test

☑ Sit an exam

☑ Report back after discussion

☑ Do a quiz

☑ Make a presentation

To ensure we have a common understanding of the terms above, read through the following brief descriptions.

Short answer or multiple-choice questions

These are examples of **objective testing**. These are tests with items to which there is only one correct answer. This means that the same marks will be given regardless of who does the marking.

Short answer items ask a closed question, for example:
What are the five characteristics of a well-written objective?

Multiple-choice items ask the learner to select the correct answer from a number of alternative options, for example:

A well-written objective has the following characteristic:

(a)   Different people can interpret it in different ways
(b)   It is written in a specific and measurable form
(c)   It defines the overall intentions of the teacher
(d)   It is written at the completion of the teaching session

(If you are wondering about the correct answer, think SMART.)

Both the above can be presented to learners either on paper or electronically, possibly using a Virtual Learning Environment (VLE) (see Chapter 9).

Observation

This involves watching learners whilst they complete a task or exercise as part of a teaching session, or during actual performance in the workplace, and noting down what you see.

It is often used in competence-based approaches to teaching. It is normal to use a standard form or checklist to ensure consistency in observation. For example:

> Observation of a learner completing a French manicure.

Project work

This involves a substantial piece of work for which learners take responsibility. It can involve a practical task or a piece of written work involving some form of research. For example:

> Learners produce a business plan for a training company.

Essay

This is a reasonably substantial piece of written work. It asks learners to show **understanding** of the subject in which they have been taught and to present reasoned arguments. For example:

> Discuss the advantages and disadvantages of the 'whole, parts, whole' method of demonstration.

Exams

These test learners' knowledge in a formal manner, either by written testing or completion of a practical task under controlled conditions. They are normally only applicable in teaching that leads to a recognised qualification, such as 'A' Level.

Oral and Aural

These assessments test speaking and listening skills. Learners are required to respond to something they listen to. They are normally used to test for understanding and are used extensively in language teaching/skills for life to test for competence.

E-assessment

Another option that is now available to us is **e-assessment**. In the same way that e-learning refers to any form of learning that is delivered electronically, e-assessment refers to the use of information technology for any assessment-related activity. You will undoubtedly be familiar with this approach as most initial assessments of numeracy and literacy take this form.

E-assessment is a rapidly developing area and can take a number of different forms; it lends itself most readily to replicating current paper testing. The candidate answers the questions electronically and this means that the test can also be marked electronically as well as manually. It does mean that questions have to be closed in nature but leads to high degrees of reliability (see later in this chapter).

The electronic medium provides a number of advantages over the paper-based approach. The use of images, sound and video clips in the test offers extra possibilities and testing can simulate 'real life' situations. Drag and drop options are also available.

Testing can be made more individual by using branching programmes whereby the answers given determine a personalised route through the test itself. If candidates are progressing well they can be directed to more difficult questions whereas those who are doing less well can be tested at a simpler and more appropriate level. E-assessment does require some ICT skills of the learner. If the learners do not have the appropriate level of functional skills this may raise problems with validity (see later in this chapter), particularly if the test is time-bound.

Purposes of assessment

We have now identified a variety of assessment methods we can use with learners. To help us to choose appropriate assessment methods, we first need to consider the specific purpose of any assessment. We need to know **why** we are assessing in order to decide how best to go about it.

You will probably have been involved in various types of assessment as a learner yourself. Drawing on this experience identify the **purpose** of each assessment below. It may help you to think about how the method was of benefit to the teacher and/or the learner.

 Activity 10.2

The purpose or benefits of the following assessment methods are:

Assessment method	Purpose/Benefit
Driving test (practical)	
Short informal quiz during a session	
Online language test prior to starting a course	
Observation of a receptionist greeting visitors	

There are many different reasons for engaging in assessment. They can be considered as falling into two main groups:

1 Assessment **of** learning. This is the type of assessment which is related to accountability. Governments (through funding bodies and inspection processes) wish to monitor standards; parents and others wish to monitor progress. Employers (through certification) want to know about competence. Learners wish to have certification to provide recognition of the level they have achieved.

2 Assessment **for** learning. The purpose of this type of assessment is to support teaching and learning. Reasonably detailed feedback is available to teachers and learners which can be used to modify teaching and learning to make it more effective.

Into which group does each of your examples from Activity 10.1 fit?

The more specific reasons for assessing learners include:

- ☑ Check learning objectives have been achieved
- ☑ Monitor learner's progress
- ☑ Correct errors in performance
- ☑ Diagnose particular areas of concern
- ☑ Predict whether learners can cope with the demands or level of programme applied for
- ☑ Provide motivation through demonstrating achievement
- ☑ Enable learners to identify their own strengths
- ☑ Provide feedback to learners
- ☑ Provide information to improve teaching/training and learning
- ☑ Inform the planning of future sessions
- ☑ Select individuals for further teaching or employment
- ☑ Recognise achievement by awarding certification

In considering our choice of assessment methods we need to be clear about what the purpose of the assessment is. For some of these purposes assessment needs to be **formal**. In other instances it can be **informal**. Formal assessment, as the name implies, will generally involve assessment results being formally recorded. Learners will know they are being assessed.

Suppose, however, that we set learners a task to perform. In their minds, it is an exercise that will help their learning or, particularly in the case of a skill, they may regard it as practice to refine their technique. Whilst they are engaged in the exercise, we can observe carefully to see if they are doing it correctly or are making mistakes. Although they do not regard this as a test, we are nonetheless assessing them, but the whole process is much less threatening. To distinguish this type of assessment from the more **formal** methods we call it **informal** assessment, the crucial difference being that learners are not aware that they are being assessed.

Both formal and informal assessments have their place in the teaching we do. Between them, they can achieve all of the purposes previously mentioned. How do you use these different forms of assessment in your own working context?

Activity 10.3

My learners undergo formal assessment when:

My learners undergo informal assessment when:

What we assess has to be placed within a context of purpose. Having considered **why** we assess, the time has now come to think about **what** it is we are assessing and **how** we will go about it.

Selecting appropriate methods

When we looked at planning a teaching session we decided the first step was to specify what we wanted our learners to learn. To do this we wrote learning objectives, detailing the learning that would be achieved. If they are **SMART** objectives then they will be written in a specific and measurable way that will give us clues about how to assess them.

Look at the following two objectives:

At the end of the session each learner will be able to:

1   Ride a bicycle safely in a straight line, unaided, for a distance of 100 metres
2   Understand how to mend a puncture in a bicycle tyre

In the box below specify how you would assess each of these objectives.

Activity 10.4

I would assess the first objective by:

I would assess the second objective by:

You will undoubtedly have found it more straightforward to arrive at an answer for the first objective. You will recognise that the first is a SMART objective and contains an action verb that gives a clear indication of the precise learning that will occur.

Consider this learning objective:

At the end of the session, each learner will be able to describe the functions of the heart

The verb in the learning objective 'describe' gives us a clue about how this could be assessed; we would need to set up conditions in which learners could 'describe'. This description could be oral or written and our choice would depend on our situation. This precise statement of learning provides us with a signpost to the most appropriate assessment method.

If the objective is imprecise, as in the second example, it is much more difficult to assess. We have to reword the objective, in our heads, into a SMART form to reach an assessment decision.

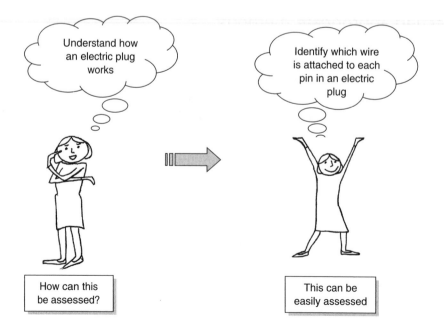

So, SMART objectives are essential to the assessment process. This in itself, however, is not sufficient; there are additional considerations to take into account.

Let us look again at a previous objective:

At the end of the session each learner will be able to ride a bicycle safely in a straight line, unaided, for a distance of 100 metres

Would you use a written test on bicycle riding to assess whether or not this objective had been achieved? To help you decide, consider whether this type of assessment actually measures what you intend it to measure – the ability to ride a bike unaided for 100 metres.

A written test on bicycle riding might allow you to test whether your learner had grasped the **knowledge** needed to ride a bicycle, but you would not know whether they could actually **ride** the bicycle for 100 metres unaided. To find this out we would have to observe learners actually riding a bike and make some judgement on how successfully they were able to do this.

Consider the learning objective:

At the end of the session, each learner will be able to order three dishes in Mandarin in a Chinese restaurant

In the following activity you are asked how you would assess this in a way that measures what you intended to measure.

Activity 10.5

I would assess the ordering of the dishes by:

In your choice of assessment you would expect an opportunity for the learner to show some oral competence. Remember, if your objective is knowledge based your assessment should check knowledge, if your objective is skill based your assessment should check skills.

Validity and reliability

The last examples illustrate one of two important qualities that all assessments must possess. We must ensure that the assessment method we choose tests the actual ability we wish it to test. In the language of assessment this is known as **validity**.

In order to produce VALID results, an assessment procedure must actually measure what we intend it to measure.

 Activity 10.6

Choose a valid method of assessment for each of the following objectives:

At the end of the session each learner will be able to:

- Replace a washer on a domestic water tap
- Express in German if you have pain or discomfort in five parts of your body
- Work out the volumes of ingredients required to mix a hair colour
- Discuss the potential impact of climate change on the Thames estuary
- Ride a bike unaided for 100 metres
- Recognise the importance of teamwork
- Evaluate the pros and cons of developing renewable energy

Having thought about what it is we want to assess and identified a method that will give us valid results, we proceed with the assessment. The next stage involves making some judgement on what has been produced. The judgement we reach should give an accurate reflection of a person's ability. Quite often this is not the case as the final decision can be influenced by a number of factors.

Consider the example we have previously used:

At the end of the session each learner will be able to ride a bicycle safely in a straight line, unaided, for a distance of 100 metres

We have agreed that in order to assess this learning we would observe the learner riding a bicycle for a distance of 100 metres. It would appear easy to make a judgement on this, but all sorts of variables may come into play and influence the judgement we reach. A further complication arises when a number of different people undertake the same assessment, possibly at the same time.

Activity 10.7

I think that the outcomes of the bicycle riding assessment could be influenced by:

There are a number of factors that could possibly influence the results of the assessment and they fall broadly under three categories: factors to do with the learners, external factors and factors to do with the assessor.

- **The learner:**
  Not feeling well, nervous about test, inappropriate frame of mind, unsure what is expected of them
- **External factors:**
  Wrong size of bicycle, different equipment from one practised on, defective equipment, bad weather conditions, road surface
- **The assessor:**
  Likes or dislikes the candidate, different assessors, concentration varies according to number of candidates, assessor not feeling well

Looking at the factors above it is evident that there are some factors over which we have some control and others over which we have none. For example, we cannot influence the health of either candidate or assessor, but we can ensure that every candidate has appropriate equipment of the same standard. These issues relate to the second key point in assessment – not only should results be valid, they should also be **reliable**.

> **The results of assessment can be considered RELIABLE if the same candidate would achieve the same result for the assessment if it were taken on another occasion or with another assessor.**

How can we ensure results that are reliable? Results should not be influenced by the occasion on which the learner takes the assessment or by our perceptions or opinions when we carry out the assessment. In other words, there must be **consistency** in the administration of the assessment procedure.

With the best intentions in the world, it is difficult, if not impossible, to achieve absolute consistency. We can, however, be more consistent by adopting a number of strategies.

In our bicycle example, our results would be more reliable if the assessor had measured the candidate's performance against a set of specific criteria. We could devise a checklist that states exactly what is required and the learner's performance can be measured against this. The more detailed and specific the checklist, the more reliable the results of our assessment will be.

Within a teaching context, all assessment decisions should be based on clear, well-defined criteria. If the assessment criteria are clear when the work is set, deciding whether a learner has met the criteria should be straightforward. More importantly, clear criteria help us to avoid bias – factors that affect the judgements made by the person doing the assessing. Bias will decrease the reliability of the assessment results. As well as helping to avoid bias in assessment decisions, knowledge of criteria will also help learners to perform better, as they will be clear as to how success will be judged.

Bias can arise in many different ways and includes anything that influences the decisions at which we arrive. It generally occurs as an unintended consequence of the actions we take within the assessment process; so we are not even aware that what we are doing will lead to bias in our judgements. What do you think might introduce bias into the assessment process?

Activity 10.8

The following may introduce bias in assessment decisions:

You may have considered the assessor being influenced by factors such as:

- The assessor's frame of mind
- The personality of the learner
- The presentation rather than the content of the work to be assessed
- The conditions under which the assessment is taking place
- Whether the learner is the first or the last to be assessed. It is likely that earlier assessments will be conducted in a different manner to later assessments
- The assessor's stereotype of the most likely candidate to succeed. This could be related to factors such as gender, age and background that we discussed in Chapter 5
- The assessor's previous experiences of the candidate. If a candidate has performed well on a previous occasion the assessor will be expecting a good performance and may judge it more favourably. The opposite can also happen. If the result is a positive bias, it is known as the 'halo' effect, whereas negative bias represents the 'horns' effect

When do we assess?

As we saw earlier, assessment has a wide range of purposes. The purpose of an assessment will have a bearing not only on how we assess, but also on when we assess. We have already looked at initial assessment in Chapter 3; now we turn our attention to our assessment of learners once they are 'on programme'.

1   At the **beginning** of a teaching session we may ask the learners questions to find out how much they know about the subject we are about to teach. This allows us to draw on experience in the group to pitch the teaching session at

the appropriate level for the learners and build upon their existing level of knowledge and skills. We could achieve this by a short written test or a quiz. Whatever the method we use, we would call this type of assessment **diagnostic**. Its purpose is to establish the presence or absence of existing knowledge and skills in addition to any knowledge we have already gained.

2   As the session progresses we continue to assess, typically by asking questions and observing learners practising what they have learned. At this stage our purpose is to check learners' progress. This helps us, as teachers, to gauge the extent of learning and to ensure the pace of learning is appropriate. For the learners it provides feedback to help them to correct mistakes, to improve upon technique and to gain some idea of the progress they are making. This type of assessment can take place at any time or times **during** the teaching session. As it helps to 'shape' the session it is termed **formative** assessment.

3   At the **end** of the teaching session, we wish to know whether the objectives for that particular session have been achieved. Again, the methods we use to do this are varied and may be formal or informal. What we seek to find out is the 'sum' total of the knowledge or skills that the learners have acquired. This type of assessment is therefore known as **summative**.

In the following activity you are asked to think of your own learners. For each heading, suggest an example of one assessment you might ask them to undertake.

Activity 10.9

I would use the following assessment methods to meet each purpose:

Purpose	Assessment method
Diagnostic	
Formative	
Summative	

It is important that both teachers/assessors and learners know how successful learning has been at all stages of teaching. The particular aspect of that success we wish to measure determines **when** – at what stage in teaching – we assess. In the above activity you selected specific assessment methods for specific purposes in your own teaching context. The information box below shows the relationship between the purpose and timing of assessment. This will influence your choice of method.

When?	Why?	Type of assessment
Beginning	To establish existing knowledge, experience or skills	Diagnostic
During	To inform both teacher and learner of progress	Formative
End	To check objectives have been achieved	Summative

Who assesses?

So far we have talked about assessment as if it is always the teacher or assessor who administers it. While this is likely to be the case most of the time, it is possible for assessment to take place without either being present. It is often difficult for the teacher to see all of the learners, spend time with individuals and give sufficient feedback. The solution to this may be to involve learners themselves in the process of assessment. This can be achieved by a variety of methods, particularly e-assessment, which can take place outside of formal teaching time, and so has the added advantage of providing an additional learning opportunity.

Learners can take part in the assessment process by assessing themselves, known as self assessment, or by assessing each other, known as peer assessment. But how can they do this if they are only just learning a procedure themselves? We can provide a checklist that lists all the stages in the procedure in the correct order. Learners can refer to the checklist in order to check their own performance (self assessment) or alternatively they may work in pairs or small groups to check each other's performance and give feedback (peer assessment). Learners could, for instance, work in a group of three:

- Learner 1 demonstrates the skill in question
- Learner 2 is used if necessary as a subject
- Learner 3 checks Learner 1's performance against the checklist
- All three learners discuss the performance of Learner 1
- The exercise can be repeated with each learner in a different role

This method also has implications for learning, as all learners will benefit from the discussion of performance. We can go around the small groups making our own observations and comments whilst this is happening. Although not all areas of assessment lend themselves easily to this approach it has considerable potential. Consider your own teaching – what possibilities are there to use either **self** or **peer assessment**?

Activity 10.10

I could use self assessment when:

I could use peer assessment when:

Designing assessments

If you are devising your own assessments you will need to consider a variety of factors we have already discussed. We have provided a checklist that will help you in designing your method of assessment.

Assessment checklist

Is the method:

☑ *Clear*
Clarity in what is being assessed and how judgements are being made

☑ *Valid*
It should assess what you really want to measure

☑ *Reliable*
Criteria and marking schemes should be clear, so that different tutors should arrive at the same result

☑ *Fair*
Learners should have equal chance to succeed even if their experiences are not identical. Literacy, numeracy, ICT or cultural aspects should be taken into account. Learners should also consider the assessment fair

☑ *Equitable*
It should not disadvantage any learner or group. Using a range of assessment methods will help

☑ *Formative*
It should enable the learner to review progress and plan further learning

☑ *Timely*
It should give early opportunities for rehearsal and feedback

---

Where do we assess?

Not all assessments can best take place in the teaching environment. Often, as for instance in NVQs, assessment is carried out in the learner's workplace. There are advantages and disadvantages if this is the case, and these will need to be considered carefully. The environment in which the assessment takes place will be influenced by what is to be assessed and how it is to be assessed. Consider this within your own teaching context in the following activity.

Activity 10.11

I think the advantages of assessing in the workplace are:

I think the limitations of assessing in the workplace are:

Some of the possible advantages you may have considered are:

- Adequate equipment is available with which the learner is familiar
- The setting is realistic
- To demonstrate some skills learners need to be working in real life situations
- The learner does not waste time travelling to an assessment centre

Whilst the possible limitations include:

- Disrupting the work procedures
- Difficult to concentrate
- Distraction from other employees

Whether we decide the most appropriate location for the assessment is the workplace or the teaching environment, we find that learners perform better if they are prepared for success. We turn our attention to this next.

Preparing learners to succeed in assessment

Whichever assessment method we choose, we want learners to perform in a manner that gives an accurate reflection of their ability. It is more likely this will happen if we prepare them to succeed. This preparation involves consideration of:

- The physical and social environment in which the assessment will take place
- The learners, ensuring they are fully aware of what to expect in an assessment and what is expected of them

The emphasis within each of these will differ depending on whether the assessment is internally or externally administered.

In the activity below you are asked how you would consider these two aspects in practice. In your consideration of an appropriate environment for assessment you may wish to refer back to ideas from 'Creating the right environment' in Chapter 2.

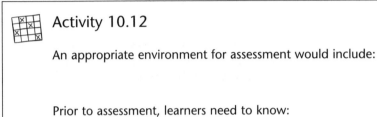

Activity 10.12

An appropriate environment for assessment would include:

Prior to assessment, learners need to know:

In terms of the environment you may have identified some of the following:

- Putting learners at ease by using first names
- Using open body language
- Arranging suitable room layout
- Checking sufficient resources are available
- Ensuring there are no unnecessary barriers to assessment

Your 'need to know' list may include:

- What is the purpose of the assessment?
- When will the assessment take place?
- How long will the assessment be?
- Which assessment methods will be used?
- What equipment and books will be allowed?
- What will marks be awarded for?
- How will results be handled and fed back to the group?

Learners will not feel adequately prepared for assessment unless they are clear about such information. Perhaps more importantly, learners are likely to perform to their potential if we help them to understand the assessment and why it is needed. This involves making the assessment criteria clear, and so helping learners to recognise exactly what it is that they need to do in order to succeed.

We can help learners to feel more confident about the assessment process if we provide opportunities for them to practise beforehand in a safe environment and give feedback on their techniques. Encouraging learners to feel relaxed and able to ask questions can also help them to feel confident and help them to perform better. This applies particularly to assessments we administer ourselves. In a formal examination setting, it is essential to adhere to regulations and a more formal code of conduct. We can also help learners to manage their time effectively and encourage them to help each other prepare for assessment. If learners feel confident about what is required of them, they will have a higher chance of success in demonstrating their achievements.

Constructive feedback

Once an assessment decision has been reached, we can consider how decisions can be conveyed to learners in a manner that will not only inform them of the outcome but will also help them learn from the experience of the assessment. To give effective feedback we should include a consideration of:

- Which criteria have been achieved
- Which criteria have not been achieved and why
- What the learner needs to do to become successful

A key consideration therefore when giving feedback is that it should be targeted to enhance learning. It should occur as soon after the assessment as possible, concentrating on what the learner should do to improve rather than being heavily judgemental. We have already looked at a model identifying the stages in giving feedback in Chapter 7. The sequence and content of feedback is not the only consideration; we need to think carefully about **how** to give feedback constructively so that learners can see its value.

Think back to occasions when you received or gave feedback. What was either positive or negative about this experience? Reflect upon these thoughts whilst you complete the next activity.

Activity 10.13

I found the following to be negative aspects of feedback:

When giving positive feedback I would consider the following:

The purpose of feedback is to help learners improve what they are doing. It follows that feedback has to be useful and given in a manner that supports the learner. The following guidelines may help you:

Giving constructive feedback:

☑ Keep the time short between performance and feedback; where possible give immediate feedback

☑ Balance negative and positive comments. Begin by thanking the learner for the work; start and end on a positive note

☑ Encourage learners to evaluate themselves. Help learners to identify what went well; aim for a dialogue

☑ Relate your feedback to the criteria set

☑ Give only two or three main points of advice; learners can soon reach information overload

☑ Offer help and make further suggestions. Concentrate on how the learner can improve in the future

☑ Distinguish between different skills, for instance they may have lots of good ideas but poor organisation

☑ Take account of the feelings of learners

☑ Feedback can be given to groups as well as individuals

If your feedback is written:

☑ Try to do more than give ticks; comments are more motivating

☑ Avoid putting crosses and too much red pen

☑ Tell learners what they have to do to improve

☑ Make your writing legible

Record keeping

Assessment is one of the most important tasks of a teacher. We must not forget to keep accurate records of this aspect of our work. There are a number of reasons for this which could be thought of as 'internal' and 'external'.

In an 'internal' sense, we need to monitor learners' progress. Any course or programme invariably contains a number of different assessment activities and the results of these need to be recorded on some form of tracking sheet. This allows us to see at a glance the progress (or lack of it) that each learner is making and informs tutorials, reviews and individual learning plans. Where we see areas of weakness common to all learners it is a signal to us to ensure that particular topic or area is consolidated and to consider how it was taught in the first instance. These records will be used internally and this relates to our earlier discussion of assessment **for** learning.

There are a number of 'external' parties who also have an interest in the achievement of learners. Parents or employers, for instance, may well want to know of progress; backing up comments with the evidence of actual marks creates a much more credible and professional impression. External verifiers and awarding bodies will require a complete audit trail of learner achievement before final certification or accreditation can be given and the only effective and reliable way to achieve this is by continuous and accurate record keeping. Records required externally are needed, as we described earlier, for assessment **of** learning.

An important aspect of quality assurance in Further Education relates to retention and achievement, as these have an impact on funding. Records of both are required to calculate achievement and success rates that will inform provision and funding for the next academic year. It is evident, then, that the recording of the results of assessment is a vital part of the teacher's role and you should bear the following in mind:

- **Be meticulous** Record marks accurately and immediately
- **Be systematic** File all records of assessment in a secure, agreed place
- **Be reliable** Pass records promptly on to the appropriate authority
- **Use technology** Produce assessment records and figures using IT

Being well organised in your assessment record keeping makes you more efficient and makes others more confident of your professionalism.

Chapter summary

The main points covered in this chapter are:

- ✓ Assessment can have a number of different purposes. Assessment methods should fulfil their intended purpose
- ✓ Assessments can be formal or informal, whereby the learner may not be aware that learning is being checked
- ✓ All assessment methods should produce results that are valid (measure what they intend to measure) and reliable (show consistency)
- ✓ Assessment can be formative (developmental) or summative (final achievement)
- ✓ With sufficient guidance, learners can assess their own work (self assessment) or the work of other learners (peer assessment)
- ✓ Assessment can be conducted within an educational setting or alternatively in the workplace
- ✓ Learners are more likely to do well in assessments if they are properly prepared
- ✓ Whether given orally or in written form, feedback should always be fair and constructive
- ✓ Recording the results of assessments is a vital part of the teacher's role

📖 Further reading

Ecclestone, K. (2005) *Understanding Assessment and Qualifications in Post-Compulsory Education and Training*, (2nd Edn). Leicester: NIACE.
This provides a deeper look at assessment and assessment issues. Chapter 1 examines purpose and types of assessment while Chapter 2 looks at the characteristics of assessment.

Huddleston, P. and Unwin, L. (2002) *Teaching and Learning in Further Education*, (2nd Edn). London: Routledge Falmer.
Chapter 6 on assessment and recording achievement looks at formative and summative approaches to assessment before giving a comprehensive overview of different methods of assessment.

Irons, A. (2008) *Enhancing Learning through Formative Assessment and Feedback*. London: Routledge.
If you want a more in-depth treatment of formative assessment this book will provide it. It also offers comprehensive coverage of giving feedback. Written for those who work in Higher Education, it provides a challenging but stimulating read.

Tummons, J. (2007) *Assessing Learning in the Lifelong Learning Sector*. Exeter: Learning Matters.
Chapter 7 gives sound advice and examples of methods of recording the results of assessment as well as the rationale behind this activity.

🖱 Useful websites

http://hotpot.uvic.ca/

www.knowledgepresenter.com/assets/home.htm

11

Exploring issues related to functional skills

> **Chapter overview**
>
> **When you have worked through this chapter on functional skills you will be able to:**
>
> - **Define functional skills**
> - **Differentiate between functional skills, basic skills and key skills**
> - **Recognise the need to develop the functional skills of learners in order to achieve learner success**
> - **Map functional skills needed by learners in your subject**
> - **Identify strategies you can use to embed functional skills in everyday teaching**

What are functional skills?

In Chapters 6–8 you considered how to support learners to acquire the knowledge, skills and attitudes related to your subject specialism. But there are other skills learners need in order to be successful in their learning.

It is likely that you have seen headlines such as:

'5 million adults in the UK cannot read the Yellow Pages'

'7 million adults cannot work out the correct amount of medicine to give a child from the label on a packet'

These adults do not have the skills to function and progress in everyday life and work; 5 million lack functional literacy; 7 million lack functional numeracy. Whilst this is indeed a problem for those individuals, it is also a major problem for the government as it is estimated that such low skills could cost the UK economy as much as £10 billion per year. The government is therefore committed to a target of improving the functional skills of 2.5 million people. However, as the Leitch report on skills (2006: para 3.30) points out, this will less than halve the problem by 2020.

This issue is also a matter of concern to LLUK (the sector skills council responsible for the teaching and learning workforce in the lifelong learning sector) which sets the national occupational standards for teachers. You are currently interested in achieving the PTLLS award and therefore moving along the path to qualified teacher status in the lifelong learning sector (QTLS). In order to gain QTLS you will be required to evidence your own functional skills at least at Level 2 (GCSE or equivalent). This requirement is part of the 'Minimum Core' for teachers within the lifelong learning sector. This obliges teachers not only to function at least at Level 2 in terms of their own literacy, numeracy and ICT ability but also to address the needs of their own learners within these areas.

So, as well as considering your own skills, you will also be expected to provide opportunities for your own learners to develop competence in speaking, listening, reading, writing, number and computer skills at the level required for their specific qualifications (see the *Minimum Core Document for the knowledge, understanding and personal skills in English, Mathematics and ICT that teachers need to undertake their professional role* www.lluk.org/documents/minimum_core_may_2007_3rdpdf).

The government launched a strategy to improve Skills for Life in 2000, defining these as follows:

> **Skills related to the ability to read, write and speak in English and to use Maths and ICT at a level necessary to function and progress at work and in society in general.**

The adult literacy, numeracy and ICT curriculum is central to the national policy and provides a map of the range of skills and capabilities that adults are expected to need.

For simplicity, all literacy, language, English, English as a second or other language (ESOL) and communications learning are described as literacy. This covers the ability to:

- Speak, listen and respond
- Read and comprehend
- Write to communicate

Similarly maths, numeracy and application of number are all described as numeracy. This covers the ability to:

- Understand and use mathematical information
- Calculate and manipulate mathematical information
- Interpret and communicate mathematical information

Similarly the ICT (Information and Communications Technology) Skills for Life standards cover the ability to

- Use ICT systems
- Find and exchange information
- Develop and present information

Depending on the qualification level and age of the learner, skills for life have variously been described by the Qualifications and Curriculum Authority (QCA) and awarding bodies as key skills, essential skills and latterly as functional skills. Some colleges choose to use the umbrella term of basic skills rather than skills for life for their provision in this area. We need to be aware that this is an area where descriptions can change rapidly! QCA is seeking to bring all these together under 'functional' skills. These have been described by QCA as 'the core elements of English, mathematics and ICT that provide an individual with the essential knowledge, skills and understanding that will enable them to operate confidently, effectively and independently in life, education and work' (see QCA website).

In arriving at this stage of this book you will have developed or used existing functional skills and have demonstrated competence in some of the Minimum Core required for QTLS. We will be using the term functional skills, without capitals, as a generic term to encompass all these skills described above, whatever label they may be given. Where we refer to the new qualifications of Functional Skills, this will be written with capital letters.

Activity 11.1

Can you recall any instance in this book where you have needed to use specific skills in literacy, numeracy or ICT?

The table on pages 161–162 summarises the current availability of frameworks for qualifications in this area.

Summary of qualification frameworks for functional skills

	Adult Literacy, Numeracy and ICT	Key Skills	GCSE	Functional Skills
Description	Laid down in National Standards for **Adult Literacy, Numeracy and ICT core curriculum** May become part of Functional Skills but can be achieved up to 2012 with last registrations in 2010	Unit-based qualifications, include **Communication, Application of number** and **ICT** Will become part of Functional Skills but can be achieved up to 2012 Currently wider Key Skills will continue to be offered (Problem solving; Working with others; Improving own learning)	Qualification within the National Curriculum for **English, Mathematics** and **ICT** A pas in Functional Skills Level 2 will be needed for GCSE (English, Mathematics and ICT) at grade C and above once revised qualifications are introduced in 2010	**English, Mathematics** and **ICT** Stand-alone qualifications, piloting in 2007/2008 Will replace Key Skills in 2010 and may replace Adult core curriculum Functional Skills will also form part of GCSEs in English, Mathematics and ICT, Diplomas (14–19) and Apprenticeship Level 2 in all three areas required for a Level 3 Diploma
Assessed by	Tests and portfolio	Tests and portfolio	Examinations and some course work	Primarily through task-based scenarios and tests but no portfolio

(Continued)

(Continued)

	Adult Literacy, Numeracy and ICT	Key Skills	GCSE	Functional Skills
Levels	Entry Levels 1–3 Levels 1–2	Levels 1–5 Levels 4 and 5 not commonly used	Grades D–F equivalent of Level 1 Grade C and above equate to Level 2 Part of the National Curriculum Key Stage 4	Entry Levels 1–3 and Levels 1–2 (Level 3 in development 2008)
Age of learners	Generally taken by adults but available for younger learners where appropriate	Mostly 16–19 but includes some adults	Mostly 14–16 but includes some 16+	Starting 14–19 but will extend to any age
Where will you find this?	In provision for adults in colleges, adult learning settings, prisons and workplace (Train to Gain for example)	As part of A level and other full-time 16–18 programmes Level 2 is a mandatory component of Apprenticeship framework, Level 3 of Advanced Apprenticeship	GCSE normally taken in Year 11 at school but may be offered as part of a re-sit programme or for adults in FE	Will be part of mainstream provision (from Key Stage 3) Mandatory in Diploma programmes: Foundation, Higher and Advanced Diplomas (for 14–19) will all contain functional skills Mandatory in Foundation Learning Tier in FE from 2010

Mapping and embedding functional skills

To read *The Sun* newspaper requires a reading age of seven. To read and digest this book requires much more advanced vocabulary and consequently a higher reading age. There is a significant relationship between the language learners can use and the development of new thinking. As you have acquired educational vocabulary it will have enabled you to analyse and reflect on your teaching in a way that you may not have been able to previously.

Literacy skills were required to understand the vocabulary in Chapter 6. For example, the word 'mnemonic' is used; this may have been new to some readers. You will then see the meaning given afterwards in more accessible language, 'memory aid'. In Chapter 10 you will have found an alternative method of stretching some readers' literacy boundaries. In this case the explanation of the concept of 'validity' comes first before what will be a new word for some readers is introduced. In these examples we have built in material that may promote new learning for you.

To meet the requirements of Level 2 in Literacy, as required by the Minimum Core for teachers, you need to:

Understand that specialist fields of knowledge, skills and interest have an associated technical vocabulary (RW.L2)

As you have worked through this book you will have encountered the specialist vocabulary associated with teaching, for example:

- The taxonomy of learning objectives in Chapter 6
- Vocabulary used in a way specific to education in the chapters related to assessment and evaluation

You may have thought, 'too much jargon!' Think about your own specialism: you will need to be able to identify and perhaps be more alert to similar reactions from your learners.

At several points in this book you have needed to understand how a graph is laid out and what the data on each axis tell you, in order to absorb the information.

Know how to interpret information from bar charts, pie charts and line graphs with more than one line (HD1.L2) Level 2 Criteria for Numeracy

In a teaching situation you should be able to spot those learners who have difficulty interpreting such information and be able to introduce other activities, related to your subject, that use this type of presentation.

An example of developing use of ICT skills can be found at the end of each chapter, where it is proposed that you access web-based material. This is in line with:

Use appropriate search techniques and design queries to locate relevant information (F1/L2:4.2) Level 2 Criteria for ICT

Obviously we cannot follow up and assess whether you can achieve this or refer you to appropriate support material. This is therefore an instance where you will need to identify your own support!

When you identify those areas in your subject where your learners will need to use specific functional skills and then find these specific competences on the associated literacy, language, numeracy or ICT curriculum, we refer to this as **mapping**. We hope you will now appreciate, from the examples above, that we have mapped the English, Maths and ICT requirements that you will face and then aimed to help you move towards achieving them through the material and activities in the book.

Making use of naturally occurring activities to help learners develop functional skills is called **embedding** functional skills; they are there, but attention is not necessarily drawn to them. Where learners receive literacy, language, numeracy and ICT support completely separately from their vocational studies the functional skills have not been integrated and are 'non-embedded'.

In this book we have embedded some requirements of the minimum core for teachers in the lifelong learning sector; the best embedding occurs when it is fully integrated and relevant to the learning goal, and hopefully that was your experience.

We would not claim to be functional skills experts and, for those of you without the Level 2 requirement in English, Maths or ICT, we have certainly not been able to embed sufficient development of skills in this book for you to meet the criteria for the Level 2 awards. However, we have tried deliberately to support such development.

Having considered initial assessment in Chapter 5 you will appreciate that you will need to review your own functional skills and whether you need to develop these; at the end of the chapter we provide suggestions for access to electronic assessment of functional skills.

Figure 11.1

Relating this to your own context

You may well be thinking, 'What does all this have to do with me as a teacher of plastering?' (or whatever your particular specialism is). Pose yourself the following questions in figure 11.1.

You are likely to have responded 'no' to these questions. This explains why achieving a certain level of functional skills is required by sector skills councils and awarding bodies as part of gaining many qualifications, why key skills are an essential component of the Apprenticeship framework and Functional Skills a mandatory part of the 14–19 diplomas.

If you intend to gain a PTLLS qualification you will already have high levels of skills in your own teaching specialism. You are not expected to be a teacher of literacy, language, numeracy or ICT but it is certainly the case that you will probably have to support some learners to develop functional skills.

In most institutions you will find a named person responsible for functional skills support. If you work in a college there is likely to be a learning support service with a focus on functional skills development. This means that you are not on your own.

- You should be able to consult a functional skills specialist when you need advice
- You will be able to refer learners to cross-college discrete functional skills programmes – literacy, language, numeracy or ICT – in which learners will be taught by functional skills specialists
- On some vocational courses arrangements can be put in place so that additional learning support is provided in your teaching environment. A functional skills specialist could work alongside you and your learners

There is scope for many naturally occurring activities in your sessions to develop functional skills within all areas of learning. You will therefore need to be able to identify opportunities for your learners to develop the increasingly higher levels of functional skills required when taking other qualifications or in the workplace. This is where functional skills experts may provide you with advice and support.

Learners can benefit from support by specialists in literacy, language, numeracy and ICT outside your teaching specialism. It is therefore important that you know what support is available to your learners and signpost this effectively to them. But there is also much that you can do, working in partnership, to ensure the success of your learners.

The government sees Level 2 qualifications as the threshold for employability. Learners with functional skills which are below Level 2 can find this lack a barrier to achievement of their goals, particularly on Level 2 vocational programmes. It is, therefore, particularly important for you as a teacher to develop awareness of the functional skills below Level 2 of the Qualifications and Credit Framework.

So what does the adult curriculum look like at lower levels?

Literacy Core Curriculum

Level	At this level someone can
Level 1	Follow a simple written procedure, fill in an application form
Entry Level 3	Obtain information on the telephone, read job adverts, write a short letter
Entry Level 2	Fill in a simple form
Entry Level 1	Follow a one-step verbal instruction, read common signs, write name and address

Numeracy Core Curriculum

Level	At this level someone can
Level 1	Read timetables, follow directions to mix substances in proportion, estimate distances on a map using scales
Entry Level 3	Use a map to find a location
Entry Level 2	Use simple measuring scales
Entry Level 1	Key in a telephone number

ICT Core Curriculum

Level	At this level someone can
Level 1	Enter, organise, develop, format and bring together information to suit context and purpose in the form of (a) text and tables, (b) images, (c) numbers, (d) records
Entry Level 3	Enter and develop information to suit purpose in the form of (a) text, (b) images, (c) numbers
Entry Level 2	Enter and edit small amounts of simple information for a simple purpose
Entry Level 1	Enter and edit simple information

Benefits of embedding functional skills

Research has been undertaken (Casey et al., 2006) to examine the impact of embedded approaches to language, literacy and numeracy. The sample consisted of 1,916 learners in health and social care, hair and beauty therapy, construction, business and engineering at Levels 1 and 2. Results showed:

- 16% better staying on rates
- more positive attitude to literacy, language and numeracy
- 26% higher success rates on Level 2 courses than those on non-embedded courses
- better achievement on literacy (up 43%) and numeracy (up 26%) qualifications than on non-embedded courses

It does have impact. Evidence suggests that vocational and functional skills specialists working together are likely to be most effective in helping learners to achieve. Work done by teachers who specialise in literacy, language, numeracy and ICT is a big part of the solution but there is much that you can do, working in partnership, to ensure the success of your learners.

However, many learners who are motivated to acquire vocational skills to access employment are much less motivated to focus on functional skills.

Activity 11.2

Why do you think this is so? (You may want to refer back to Chapter 5 on motivation in order to respond.)

Let us take the example of Key Skills provision which can be a mandatory part of 'A' level and other programmes. Many learners have negative attitudes towards Key Skills either because they cannot see the relevance or have previously experienced failure in this area. Some learners consider practical experience to be more important; this affects their motivation. Whilst learners may realise that they will need to communicate effectively when at work, to deal with customers, they are not at all convinced of the particular value of functional skills development. It is possible that these negative attitudes to functional skills can be reinforced if not dealt with in an appropriate manner.

The government is increasingly focused on developing the vocational skills of those in employment and here a similar issue arises. Individuals may be keen to gain vocational skills but less willing to admit inadequacies in functional skills, particularly when they may have hidden such deficiencies for years. Again, embedded functional skills development is important in achieving success in workplace National Vocational Qualifications (NVQs).

Hopefully the discussion above has started you thinking about how you could embed functional skills related to English, Maths and ICT in the teaching of your subject.

Case Study

On a Painting and Decorating course, the teacher worked with a functional skills specialist to produce an integrated assignment. The assignment was in four parts; an extract from this is given below.

This enabled learners to achieve the performance criteria of their NVQ and at the same time to meet elements of the core curriculum/Key Skills.

Assignment

Part C:
Describe an accident using an Accident Report Form

NVQ ref	Performance criteria	Core curriculum refs	Core curriculum elements
VRO1.4	Comply with all emergency procedures in accordance with organisational policy	Wt.L2.2	Judge how much to write and the level of detail to include Present information and ideas in a logical sequence Use format and structure to organise writing for different purposes Follow and contribute to discussions on a range of straight-forward topics

Part D:
Make a list of people who would be involved in investigating an accident

NVQ ref	Performance criteria	Core curriculum refs	Core curriculum elements
VRO1.4	Comply with all emergency procedures in accordance with organisational policy	Wt/L1.5	Use format and structure for different purposes Present information and ideas in a logical sequence and provide further detail and development to clarify or confirm understanding

Key Skills:
Successful completion of this assignment will cover the following Key Skills:
Part A and C – Level 1 C1.3 Write two different types of documents
Part B and D – Level 2 C2.2 Read and summarise ... C2.1b Give a short talk ...

DfES, 2005 Materials for Embedded Learning

Activity 11.3

Thinking of your subject specialism:
Identify instances within the teaching of your subject when learners can demonstrate competence in literacy, numeracy or ICT through a task or practical activity

Think of a new activity where you could incorporate more than one of these functional skills into a subject related task?

To have the maximum impact in your approach to functional skills it is worth considering the following success factors:

Success factors
Learners
☑ Get to know your learners
☑ Do not assume competence from any level of learner for literacy, language, numeracy or ICT
☑ Make full use of initial assessment and induction to produce individual learning plans
☑ Use multi-sensory lessons because the more senses involved the more you can tap into learners' preferences
☑ Think how things can be explained as simply as possible
☑ Discuss links between functional skills development, vocational success and personal aspirations

If working with specialist functional skills staff
☑ Develop strong working relationships with staff teaching language, literacy, numeracy or ICT and arrive at a shared understanding of the value of functional skills
☑ Ensure specialist functional skills staff understand the demands of the vocational course and its vocabulary
☑ Encourage an awareness in specialist staff of learners' vocational goals
☑ Promote aspects of teaching and learning that connect functional skills to vocational content

---

In your organisation

- ☑ Find out about your organisation's approach to functional skills
- ☑ If you are planning induction make sure your learners are fully aware of the support available
- ☑ Try to timetable functional skills so that the subject is adjacent to vocational skills, not on a different day
- ☑ Take up training opportunities to develop your teaching of functional skills

---

All this will demonstrate your commitment to functional skills. Working alongside specialist functional skills staff you will be helping learners to achieve their full potential.

Chapter summary

The main points covered in this chapter are:

- ✓ Functional skills are the core elements of English, Mathematics and ICT that enable individuals to function effectively and independently in life, education and work
- ✓ Different titles are used for this area of work
- ✓ A learner with good functional skills is more likely to be successful on their chosen vocational or academic programme
- ✓ Mapping involves analysing the specific functional skills needed to succeed on a learning programme.
- ✓ Embedding requires you to make use of naturally occurring activities in your subject specialism to help learners develop functional skills
- ✓ Working in partnership with functional skills specialists enables you to integrate functional skills development in the teaching situation
- ✓ Awareness of learning support available in your institution allows you to be effective in signposting learners to this
- ✓ You can use the checklist of success factors above

→ References

Casey, H. et al. (2006) *'You wouldn't expect a maths teacher to teach plastering ...' Embedding Literacy, Language and Numeracy on Post-16 Vocational Programmes – the Impact on Learning and Achievement.* London: NRDC.

Leitch, S. (2006) *Prosperity for All in the Global Economy – World Class Skills.* London: HMSO (see www.hm-treasury.gov.uk/leitch)

LLUK. www.lifelonglearning.uk

 Further reading

Skills for Business (2007) *Addressing Literacy, Language, Numeracy and ICT Needs in Education and Training: Defining the Minimum Core of Teachers' Knowledge, Understanding and Personal Skills.* London: LLUK.

⌒🖱 Useful websites

Further information about **Skills for Life**: the national strategy for improving literacy and numeracy skills:

www.dcsf.gov.uk/readwriteplus

To receive a quarterly Skills for Life update email:

asflupdate@prolog.uk.com

QCA
For links to the Functional Skills standards:

www.qca.org.uk/functionalskills

Move on
For an online introduction to Skills for Life – iRoute, case studies, access to free resources and a GOAW section with staff development for designing and delivering a contextualised programme to meet workplace needs:

www.move-on.org.uk

For skills checklists that can be customised to show relevance to a sector or workplace:

www.move-on.org.uk/moveonguides/intermediaries

Functional Skills Support Programme (FSSP)

www.lsneducation.org.uk/functionalskills

QIA Excellence Gateway
This site includes Managing Delivery – Teaching and Learning Functional English; Functional Mathematics and Functional ICT; and a presentation on Functional Skills for adults (June 2008):

www.excellence.qia/org.uk/functionalskills

National Centre for Excellence in the Teaching of Mathematics

Leading on a national post-16 numeracy strategy: Numeracy for Employability

www.ncetm.org.uk

Embedding support package for Skills for Life Improvement

Program website:

www.sflip.org.uk

www.dfes.gov/uk/readwriteplus/embeddedlearning

12

Developing session plans

Chapter overview

When you have worked through this chapter on developing session plans you will be able to:

- Recognise the three functions of a session plan
- Identify what should be included in a plan
- manage time better
- Describe the different phases of a teaching session and what is included in each
- Self-evaluate a teaching session in a systematic manner
- Identify session formats appropriate to either a group or workshop setting

---

The purpose of planning

We have already agreed that normally, whatever we do, we do it better if we plan it first. Planning is part of our everyday life. If we go on a trip, we first get out the appropriate map and plan our route. If we go shopping, we first write a list of the things we need to buy. If we want to build a house, we first draw up the appropriate plans. Similarly any form of teaching, whether it be a theoretical, practical or attitudinally based subject, works better if we first draw up a plan of our intentions.

The word **intentions** is important here because a plan is what we draw up before the event. It maps out what we anticipate will happen. If we put some thought into this and consider all the different factors that will affect the plan, then our intentions and what happens on the day should be fairly close. Often, however, events take a turn which we could not have anticipated.

Activity 12.1

What unexpected events or conditions might mean you have to depart from a session plan?

Typically some of the following may occur:

- The learners know more or less than we thought
- The learners are held up and arrive late for the session
- The resources we require are unavailable
- Someone comes up with a good idea that is worth pursuing

Do we ignore these or do we take these into account? Let us consider our other examples of planning. If we started off on our journey and found there was heavy traffic on our intended route, would we sit in it because our original plan said that was our route? We could do, but it would be much more sensible to adapt our planned route to meet these unexpected circumstances. Similarly, if we were building a house we may alter our plans to take advantage of new building materials that have been developed, rather than stick to the old materials just because they were on our original plan.

Plans we write for teaching, then, are not scripts that must be followed to the letter. Plans are guidelines that can be used flexibly to ensure a more effective session. We will explore the idea of flexibility further as we progress through this chapter. First we need to identify our purpose in writing these plans.

Session plans have three functions that refer to different stages of the teaching process:

Before

By writing a session plan, we are prepared and confident before we teach. Even if it is a new area of teaching for us, when we come to deliver it for the first time we have already delivered it 'in our head'. The session plan contains a list of all of the resources we need. By reference to it we can be confident we have everything ready.

During

The session plan is a checklist, not only of resources, but also of what you are to deliver and how. It provides a memory aid of all aspects of the delivery of the session which you can refer to at any stage. It helps us to stick to the 'best' sequence, reminds us of the main points we wish to make and helps us to manage time. Generally, it ensures that, as far as circumstances allow, we deliver the session as we had intended.

After

If you repeat a teaching session, will you start from scratch in your planning? Not if you have a record of a previous occasion that you can refer back to. This is the third function of the session plan; it provides you with a record of what you have done. When you plan this session again you can look back to this previous session and use the same plan again, or you can change it to fit the demands of the new context. You may make changes based on your experience of the previous occasion. This is a notion we will pursue further when we look at evaluation.

There are two factors that are important with regard to this 'after' function:

1   You will need more detail on a lesson plan than is necessary just to deliver it in the 'during' phase if the plan is to be an effective record. Key words may trigger thoughts whilst the plan and its contents are still fairly fresh in your mind, but if you come to teach the same or a similar session at a later stage, maybe six months or a year later, this will undoubtedly not be the case. The plan needs sufficient detail to be able to act as a 'stand-alone' record that does not rely in part on memories of the session.
2   It is important, early on in your teaching career, to develop a system for storing the session plans you write. If you do this electronically it will allow you to 'cut and paste' between different plans and add to or alter existing plans; recycling is a current concern and when applied to teaching plans, allows us to derive the greatest return from the efforts we have made in writing them in the first place.

Planning decisions

The plan is a record of the decisions we have arrived at in planning that particular session.

Your decisions will cause you to ask the following sorts of questions when you are planning:

* Where will the session take place?
* How many learners will there be?
* What do they already know, what can they already do?
* What are the aims and objectives of the session?
* Are they relevant and realistic to the learners?
* What information will I have to impart?

- How much time can I spend on each topic?
- What methods will I be using?
- What resources are available?
- How can I check that learning has occurred?
- How will I know if the session has been successful?

You will see that there are lots of questions to answer and too many decisions to be made for you to remember. This is especially difficult when you are delivering the session and your attention is occupied by more immediate concerns; this information is therefore best recorded. The act of recording it also helps you to put a structure on your thoughts and decisions. This allows you to be more systematic in your approach to planning.

 Activity 12.2

Is there anything else you would want to include on a plan?

Having decided what to record, the next consideration is the format or layout of the plan.

Structuring a session plan

Possibly you have a lesson plan format that your employing institution either advises or requires you to use or perhaps your PTLLS course has a recommended format, but ideally you are in a position whereby you can devise a plan to fit your own particular circumstances and preferences. Individual session plans are taken from a scheme of work, which in turn is a breakdown of the syllabus to which you will be working. At this stage we are only concerned with planning at session level and so you will find it helpful to look at the example session plans on pages 176–77 and 185. The first of these is the type of format that would be used when teaching a group, probably in a classroom setting. Quite often, however, although we have a group of learners, they could be working independently on individual projects, possibly in a workshop setting; the second format suggests how planning might be recorded in this type of situation.

You will notice that the sample plans using Format 1 record two types of information. The first page relates to the context of the session and the second to its delivery.

Format 1 – Group plan

Course:		Group:	
Venue:		Time:	Date:
Topic/Title:		Aims:	
Learning outcomes:		How each outcome will be assessed:	Checklist of resources required:
Notes on learners:	Differentiation strategies:		Links to functional skills:
Self-evaluation:			

Time	Development	Delivery		Resources	Assessment
		Teacher activity	Learner activity		
	Introduction				
	Middle				
	End				

The context of the session

- Where and when the session will be conducted
- What is to be learned (objectives) and how it is to be assessed
- The main resources required
- Who the learners will be and any particular characteristics of individual learners or the group as a whole that need to be considered
- Differentiation strategies to be employed
- Any functional skills needs
- The resources required
- What has been learned as a result of teaching this session

The context is concerned mainly with the '**Before**' and '**After**' functions of the session plan. **Before** it encourages you to think about the objectives of the teaching session, the learners who are to achieve these and how you propose to check that learning is indeed taking place as the session proceeds. You will want to write SMART objectives that are achievable and relevant to your learners and ensure that the session is inclusive in its planning. The plan also demonstrates how you have considered the functional skills needs of both your subject and your learners. The checklist of resources helps ensure you have everything you need. What you record in the section on self-evaluation informs the planning of future sessions and so also fulfils an **After** function. The **During** functions are mainly to do with the delivery on the day and we shall look at these issues next.

The delivery of the session

You will find the following items related to the delivery of the teaching session on the example plans:

- Timing
- The development of content and the sequence in which it will be delivered
- The activities employed at each stage of the session
- When and how learning resources will be used
- Checks on learning

Decisions concerning these items are best recorded in columns on a session plan as this makes it easier for you to focus on the specific items you require. We will look at some of these in more depth.

Timing

Time is the most precious commodity in a teaching session. There is rarely sufficient time to cover all you want, in the depth you wish. So, as with any other precious commodity, what time is available should be put to best use. We manage this by allocating blocks of time to each area to be covered.

Often our estimates of time will not be as accurate as we would like, particularly if we are dealing with a new topic. Consider the following sequence:

```
 9.30   Introduction

 9.40   Activity 1

10.05   Activity 2

10.30   Break

10.45   Activity 3

11.20   Draw conclusions

11.30   End
```

What happens if the introduction overruns and we do not start Activity 1 until 9.50? Activity 2 then takes until 10.45 and our times are already inaccurate. How can we retrieve the situation? Actually, this is not disastrous by any means. Sticking to the times is not our key concern; our main priority is that learners achieve the objectives. There are only two times that have to be strictly observed: the **Start** time and the **Finish** time. If this is so, why write the other times on the plan?

Suppose you go on a journey of 100 km which you have to complete in two hours. You start off at the allocated time and find that you reach the halfway point in only 45 minutes. You now know that if you complete the journey at the same speed, you will arrive 30 minutes early. You have the option then, of travelling more slowly or altering your plans and taking a more 'scenic route'. Alternatively if you find you have taken 75 minutes to reach the halfway point, you know that you will not arrive at your destination in time if you carry on at that speed. You will have to go faster or find a shorter route to arrive at your destination on time. In both cases it is important that you are aware of the situation when there is still an opportunity to respond. If you do not find out until the end of the journey, you are not in a position to do anything about it.

A similar argument applies to the times on session plans. These can be compared to 'distance markers' rather than deadlines to be adhered to. By being aware of whether we are behind time, on time or ahead of time at any stage during the session, we can adjust our pace and delivery so we can stick to those two important times of **Start** and **Finish**. The purpose of recording times on a plan is to enable more effective and flexible management of time, not to provide a timetable that must be rigidly followed.

One way of achieving this is by classifying the content of the session in terms of relative importance and we often use the categories of that which learners 'must know', 'should know' and 'could know' to accomplish this.

- **'Must know'** refers to material that is essential to the achievement of the learning objectives and preserving this is a priority in all adjustments we make.
- **'Should know'** is useful because it elaborates or extends the 'must know' category. Every effort should be made to cover this material but if our timing goes seriously wrong, we will consider leaving it out to preserve the 'must know'.

- **'Could know'** might be helpful to the learners because it illustrates or extends the previous categories, but it is not essential to achievement of the learning objectives. It is the sort of material we will include if time permits but we will leave it out if we have to in favour of the other, more important categories.

Timing the delivery of sessions improves with practice; classifying the material we intend to include in the session allows us to be flexible with our timing, ensuring essential points are covered and we respond to the needs of learners more effectively.

Content and order

It is useful to think of sessions having a **Beginning – Middle – End** pattern. We will consider each part of this structure in turn.

The **Beginning** of the session is where we make our initial impact and set the scene for what is to follow. Exactly what is included at this stage will depend upon factors such as:

- Is this a 'one-off' session or part of a sequence?
- Do you know the learners and do they know you?
- Are learners familiar with the environment?

There are, however, a number of features that we might expect to see in a Beginning.

Activity 12.3

I think the following should take place at the beginning of a session:

In general, the following might be included in a Beginning of a 'one-off' session or a first meeting between you and the group:

Introductions

- Introduce yourself – give a little relevant background to establish credibility
- Give the learners an opportunity to introduce each other

Practical matters

- Give the location of any appropriate facilities
- Explain any Health and Safety requirements and show Fire Exits
- Complete any necessary paperwork

Setting the scene

- Introduce the topic – what will be covered (or possibly not covered)
- Show how it links to what learners already know
- Introduce any ground rules – acceptable procedures for this session

Arousing interest

- Explain the relevance and benefits of the teaching you will be delivering
- Present an enthusiastic role model

If you and the group already know each other and the session is part of a sequence, a more likely procedure would be:

1 Involve learners straight away with an active start to the session – a short, sharp exercise can be given to learners as they enter the room which is sufficiently flexible in its layout to allow you to stop it at a convenient moment; perhaps a 'gap-fill' exercise or quiz which involves a recap of the previous session. This allows you to integrate latecomers into the session with minimum disruption and affords an opportunity for some initial individual contact.
2 Bring the exercise to a halt and acknowledge the work that has been completed before formally recapping previous learning, perhaps using question and answer. Next outline the proposed outcomes of the session, their relevance and usefulness and the types of activities that are to be used.

The **Middle** of the session covers the delivery of the main content and introduces any activities or exercises that are planned. The content should be delivered in a logical sequence and preferably be split into smaller sub-sections.

In general, new information should build on existing knowledge and experience. Learners take in information most easily if a basic, simple idea is introduced to start off with that can then be built up to a higher level of complexity.

As seen in Chapter 6, attention spans tend to be longer when more 'active' teaching methods are employed. Conversely, teaching methods where learners take a more 'passive' role are less effective in attracting and maintaining attention. Although the level of attention will normally fall to some degree as the session progresses, a variety of methods is important in maintaining attention and concentration levels at their highest levels. This could be achieved through a sequence such as:

1 Initial explanation and introduction of new material with some question and answer
2 Some form of exercise/group work/pair work using the new material
3 Learning check, summary and link to the next stage of the session
4 Repeat a similar pattern until the session objectives are achieved

This pattern can be adapted to suit your own style but, when supported by appropriate resources, should suit most circumstances.

Endings, like Beginnings, often include a number of common features.

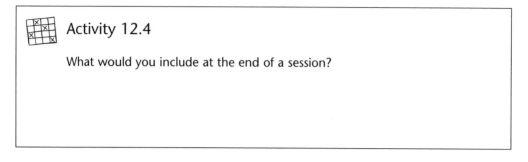

Activity 12.4

What would you include at the end of a session?

The End of the session is where all of the threads are drawn together and the important points highlighted. In ending a session, you might:

- Review the session as a whole
- Ask questions on the main points covered
- Take any questions on matters arising out of the session
- Suggest follow-up exercises
- Show how this session links with future sessions

Considering the sequence and content of a session enables us to develop a sound structure for the delivery of our teaching.

Self-evaluation

Sometimes a session goes well and sometimes, despite our best efforts, it does not. Whichever the case might be, we can learn from every session we deliver and use that learning to improve future sessions. We achieve this through a process of evaluation.

Evaluation can be defined as:

> **The collecting of information about the sessions we deliver that allows us to make informed decisions concerning our teaching, leading to the improvement of future sessions**

Information necessary for evaluation can be obtained from a number of sources:

- Yourself
- Your learners
- Colleagues

And by a number of means:

- Self-rating checklists – used by you after completing a session
- Oral feedback – individual and group discussion with learners or colleagues

- Written feedback – evaluation sheets completed by learners
- Checklists completed by colleagues

Most often, however, the kind of evaluation we engage in is self-evaluation when, after the session, we would ask ourselves a number of questions and record our answers on the lesson plan. This acts as a reminder of how this session went and what we have learned from the experience that can inform our planning if we deliver this, or a similar session again. The kind of questions we would ask ourselves are:

1 What were the significant features of this session? Which parts of it were well received? Which parts of the session proved difficult or generally didn't go so well?
2 Why? What were the reasons behind the more and less successful aspects of the session?
3 If these are the reasons, what might I do differently next time I teach either this session or this group?

Sometimes, prior to the session, we might have an idea of specific aspects that it would be useful to evaluate, giving our self-evaluation a more structured approach.

Activity 12.5

What areas would you find it useful to consider in your self-evaluation?

Self-evaluation contributes to the **After** function of the session plan when it acts as a record of what has been done. When we come to deliver this or a similar session again we know not only what we planned to do, but also how effective this was, and we are in a better position to think through any changes that might be appropriate next time.

We have now considered in some detail what to think about when constructing a session plan and how to record these decisions. To help you in writing your own plans, you might find it useful to refer to the checklist below.

Session Plan Checklist
Does your plan contain the following?

☑ Well-stated learning objectives
☑ An indication of differentiation strategies to be used
☑ Identification of functional skills related to this topic
☑ Clear introduction
☑ Logical progression
☑ Timing
☑ Variety of appropriate teaching methods and learning activities
☑ Plenty of learner participation
☑ Variety of appropriate resources
☑ Checks on learning
☑ Something to leave out or add in

Planning format for a project or workshop

In a project or workshop situation, although you may start and end the session by addressing the group as a whole, learners will be working individually for the vast majority of the time. The exact nature of their learning will depend upon the task or activity in which they are engaged. Outcomes, activities, assessment and resources will vary from learner to learner and so planning has to take account of this. Format 2 (page 185) provides a way of planning which is personalised and takes account of the needs of each individual learner. The top line gives some context but the plan is mainly concerned with identifying individual targets and tracking progress.

In the case of Learner 1, the plan would be filled in as follows:

- The **date is** the date of the particular session.
- The **outcome/target** box is used to record whatever it is that the individual learner is to achieve in the session. It can be phrased as a learning outcome, a task, a series of short tasks or a short-term goal, depending upon which of these is more appropriate to the kind of session being run. Whatever the choice, it should provide Learner 1 with a sense of purpose and a structure to work from and can be reviewed as the session progresses.
- Towards the end of the session, time needs to be made to meet briefly with each learner and review progress. At this stage an entry is made in the **progress/ evaluation** box, summarising either what has been learned, progress with the task, obstacles encountered and overcome, or whatever is deemed appropriate. The purpose here is to evaluate performance and identify what has been learned. This entry can be made by learners or jointly, depending upon level of maturity and independence.
- The outcome/target for the next session can also be agreed and recorded at this stage, so learners know what they will be doing in advance and you will be aware of any resource implications which can be recorded in the resources for the next session box.

Format 2 – Workshop plan

	Course:	Module:	Venue:
	Date:	Date:	Date:
Learner 1	Outcome/Target:	Outcome/Target:	Outcome/Target:
	Resource requirements:	Resource requirements:	Resource requirements:
	Progress/Evaluation:	Progress/Evaluation:	Progress/Evaluation:
Learner 2	Outcome/Target:	Outcome/Target:	Outcome/Target:
	Resource requirements:	Resource requirements:	Resource requirements:
	Progress/Evaluation:	Progress/Evaluation:	Progress/Evaluation:

Case Study

Learner 1 comes into the plumbing workshop. An outcome has been agreed the previous session, so Learner 1 knows what is to be done in this session. Learner 1's first task is to identify the tools required for the job. When the tool list is prepared, it is checked with the teacher or technician, and tools are issued to Learner 1. Teacher then checks what learner proposes to do and gives the 'go ahead' to start work. The teacher monitors progress	**Outcome/target:** **Install Radiators Bay 4** Hang radiators on wall. Connect flow and return pipe work. Test and balance radiators
	Resource requirements: Prepare tool list. List materials including type and size of radiator valves
Shortly before the end of the session, the teacher discusses progress with Learner 1 and they agree the outcome/target for the next session and record this on the next section of the plan	**Progress/Evaluation:** Radiators hung correctly although getting them level took longer than expected Continue with pipe work and testing next session

Following weeks look like this:

Outcome/Target: Continue piping and testing of radiators	**Outcome/Target:** Check standards for clip spacing Fill radiators ready for testing and marking
Resource requirements: List of copper tube and fittings required	**Resource requirements:** Current standards for testing information. Clips to be ordered for stores – state how many you will need
Progress/Evaluation: Radiators piped up with correct valves and size of pipe. A few more clips are required to comply with current standards. As soon as this is done we are ready for testing	**Progress/Evaluation:** Installation completed correctly. Very neat job. One small water leak, which was repaired promptly. Pipe work connected to boiler. Radiators balanced and working correctly. Job photographed and stripped out Ready to progress to water cylinder activity next session

As learners become familiar with the process, they can become more involved in the planning of their own learning and possibly reach a stage when the process can be handed over to them.

In the workplace Learner 1 will have to plan what is to be achieved in the morning or by the end of the day in order to work effectively and cost jobs accurately. By encouraging learners to negotiate and reflect on what they want to achieve we contribute towards the development of this skill as well as giving learners some control over their learning.

You should now be able to produce a well-structured session plan to use in your teaching, whether as a whole group or for individuals. The suggested formats can be changed and adapted to meet your own specific needs and further developed as you become more familiar with the processes and demands of planning. Further examples, which have been completed, are provided in Appendix 2.

Planning does improve with practice!

Chapter summary

The main points covered in this chapter are:

- ✓ Plans record our **intentions** for a particular session
- ✓ Session plans have three functions – Before, During and After – and the requirements of each influence how we complete the plan
- ✓ Session plans record both the context within which a session occurs and the intended strategy to be adopted
- ✓ Timings on a session plan act as reference points rather than as a timetable
- ✓ A well-structured session contains a defined Beginning, Middle and End, each of which has a specific purpose
- ✓ Self-evaluation is the process of reviewing all aspects of the planned session with a view to improvement
- ✓ Different planning formats are used for whole group and workshop settings

---

Further reading

A number of general texts cover planning. Two of these are:

Le Versha, L. and Nicholls, G. (2003) *Teaching at Post 16*. London: Kogan Page.
Chapter 8 gives a planning format and discusses a number of planning issues, particularly differentiation.

Reece, I. and Walker, S. (2007) *Teaching Training and Learning: A Practical Guide*, (6th Edn). Sunderland: Business Education Publishers.
Some useful background on planning and some other formats for consideration in the section on 'Planning Learning' in Chapter 1.

Sotto, E. (2007) *When Teaching Becomes Learning*, (2nd Edn). London: Continuum.
Chapter 17 looks at session planning and ties this in with assessment and evaluation.

13

Evaluating and reviewing

Chapter overview

When you have worked through this chapter on evaluating and reviewing you will be able to:

■ Define evaluation
■ Identify the purposes of evaluation
■ List different methods to evaluate sessions and recognise strengths and limitations of each
■ Recognise the characteristics of a well-written questionnaire
■ Draw up a personal action plan to improve your future sessions

---

Why evaluate?

When we assess, we are looking to see whether or not objectives have been achieved. Evaluation, whilst taking account of the results of assessment, also takes a wider view of the delivery of learning. The word evaluation relates to **value** and is concerned with questions about the worth and value of a session or programme and how it has been conducted.

When we evaluate we are looking for the answers to questions such as:

• Were the objectives appropriate and achievable?
• Were the methods selected suitable, matching both objectives and learner characteristics?
• Was the pacing of the session right?
• Were the resources used the most appropriate, and if so, were they used to best advantage?
• Was learning checked using appropriate formal or informal methods?

The example below concerns people learning Mandarin to conduct business meetings in China; we can easily see from this how the assessment and evaluation processes complement each other.

Assessment at the end of the course will tell us whether or not learners can ask simple questions and give simple explanations which will be understood in China.

Evaluation might further inform us that the learners wanted more time to talk, that they would have liked sessions to be livelier, with more work in pairs, and that they felt they could have benefited from extra study between sessions.

The key purpose of evaluation (previously defined on page 182) is to enable us to **gather information** that gives a measure of the **effectiveness** of the delivery of learning. We can then **use** this information **to improve** future sessions or programmes that we conduct. So, evaluation often leads to:

- changes in the design of the teaching or training we offer
- changes in the way we deliver learning

Evaluation therefore involves looking back over a session or programme. We gather as much evidence as we can in order to weigh up how it has gone – what its strengths and weaknesses were – with the intention of making it better next time.

The questions we have posed above are very general in nature; in order to bring about meaningful improvement we would need to consider more specific areas related to our own teaching and learning context.

Activity 13.1

What specific areas would be of particular interest to you when evaluating your own teaching?

How does your list compare with the areas for evaluation that we have identified below?

- Did learners achieve the objectives?
- Content of your programme – was it relevant to the learners' work situation?
- Programme objectives – were they appropriate and SMART?
- Planning – did it take account previous experience and level of understanding?

- Suitability of the facilities
- Use of visual aids and other resources
- Sequencing of materials
- Pacing of delivery
- Balance of learner and teacher activity
- Degree of learner participation
- Group management
- Responsiveness to learner needs
- Issues of equality
- Appropriate communication patterns
- Level of rapport with learners
- Suitability of methods of delivery
- Attention level of learners
- Sufficient opportunities for practice
- Appropriate methods of checking learning
- Quality of feedback given to learners

How to evaluate

What methods of evaluation can we use?
In order to help us identify which methods of evaluation we could use, think back to sessions or programmes in which you have been involved as a learner. How do you think the teacher could have made a judgement on the success of the session or programme? What sources of information were available to them?

 Activity 13.2

The teacher could judge the success of the programme by:

The sources of information available to the teacher were:

The following are some possible sources of information:

- Talking to learners
- Written feedback – participant questionnaire
- Enrolment numbers
- Level of participation
- How many learners drop out of the programme
- Feedback from an observer
- Discussion
- Attendance
- Arrival times
- Assessment results
- Peer evaluation

All of these give us an indication of how the programme is progressing or has progressed. We will, of course, be forming an impression (known as formative evaluation) as we go along by informal means such as:

- The expressions on learners' faces
- Eye contact or lack of it
- How people sit – forward or back
- The degree of learner participation
- The level of enthusiasm within the group

These only give us impressions, however, and we normally rely on formal methods to obtain more reliable information. These formal methods tend to be used at the end of a session or programme in a summative manner.

We have already touched upon **self-evaluation** in Chapter 12, where we reflect upon our own performance. This is a necessary activity for anyone who wishes to improve their effectiveness as a teacher. Self-evaluation can, however, be rather narrow in scope as it focuses on areas viewed only from the teacher's personal perspective. A more revealing process is to ask the learners for feedback and this can form the basis for formal evaluation of sessions and programmes. We will examine this in more detail before briefly returning to self-evaluation at the end of this section.

To obtain the information we require, we can either ask learners directly for their opinions – spoken techniques – or have them fill in some form of evaluation questionnaire – written techniques. Each technique has its own particular advantages and drawbacks. We shall consider each in turn.

Spoken techniques
It is possible for us to talk to learners individually but this is generally a time-consuming process. We are, therefore, more likely to use some form of group technique. This has the further advantage of interaction, which may encourage learners to feed off and build upon each other's comments. There are, however, potential problems with spoken techniques.

Activity 13.3

I think the potential problems of using spoken techniques of evaluation are:

You may have identified some of the following problems as ones you may encounter in using spoken evaluation techniques:

Content

- Discussion centres on limited areas

Contributions

- Everyone talks at once
- Individuals take over the evaluation
- Some learners make no contribution at all
- We assume that individuals are talking on behalf of the group as a whole

These problems can be largely offset by the way in which we conduct the evaluation.

Content

Often discussion can become narrow in focus or alternatively can jump from one topic to another. It helps to have some form of structure within which to work. We can broaden the discussion and help it keep focus by identifying the range of areas to be covered in advance.

To achieve this we can pose specific questions or nominate particular topics to be covered. Alternatively, we can ask our learners to come up with some headings that will provide a structure. Often a good compromise is to use a combination of our own and learners' suggestions. Some learner participation in proposing discussion areas is desirable, to overcome the bias that we, as teachers, might otherwise impart to proceedings.

Contributions

We can employ a variety of discussion techniques to try to counter the problems identified above. You were introduced to some of these in Chapter 8 but they are used slightly differently for evaluation purposes. These will include the following:

Snowballing

In this activity we first ask learners to jot down their thoughts on the course individually on a piece of paper. They then discuss these with one other member of the group. Pairs then combine and discuss in fours. This 'doubling up' can be repeated as many times as we think appropriate and will be determined to a large extent by the size of the group as a whole. The final groups each elect a spokesperson to feed back the conclusions of their discussion. This method ensures that everyone contributes to the final evaluation and the appointment of a spokesperson depersonalises the process of giving feedback.

A round

We ask each learner in turn for a contribution. To make this exercise less threatening we can allow learners to 'pass' when their turn comes around, although to some extent this defeats the purpose of having everyone make a contribution to the evaluation.

Buzz groups

We split the larger group into a series of smaller groups. The course experience is discussed in these groups and their conclusions are reported back by the nominated spokesperson at the end of the evaluation.

It is very important that we keep some record of the discussion. Ideally this should be a 'public' record that could be copied and distributed.

Written techniques

Spoken techniques can be very time-consuming and often we make use of written techniques because they are quicker and easier to administer. Written techniques can lead to more honest feedback, as learners may well feel able to commit to paper what they feel unable to tell us face to face. This is particularly the case if learners can respond anonymously. The most frequently used written technique is the questionnaire. There are a number of ways in which we can design a questionnaire. This will depend on whether our main aim is to collect detailed information or to collect information that we can easily collate and analyse.

In the following example you will find different questions we could ask if we wanted you, our readers, to evaluate the section so far.

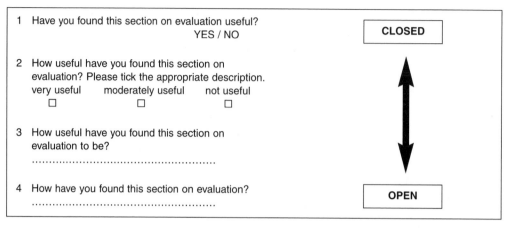

From the examples in the diagram you can see that questions can be closed in nature, requiring only a straightforward 'yes' or 'no', or open-ended, encouraging a detailed response. The first question is the most closed and the last the most open. Closed questions provide us with limited information, but have the advantage that we can collate the responses easily. We would be more likely to use this type of question if we had a large number of questionnaires. The last question is the most open and therefore provides a rich, detailed source of data. This does mean, however, that it can be difficult to collect all the responses together.

Often we use a combination of question types, the first to elicit a simple response and the second to seek further clarification if required:

---

1 Has this section on evaluation been relevant to your own teaching situation?

YES / NO

2 If not, please say why and suggest how it could have been improved.

Whatever type of question we use, the devising and writing of evaluation questionnaires requires careful thought. The following points provide some guidance:

When writing questionnaires remember to:
- ☑ Keep questions simple and concise
- ☑ Leave sufficient space for answers
- ☑ Make the layout consistent
- ☑ Make the design attractive
- ☑ Limit the number of questions
- ☑ Ask easier questions first
- ☑ Cover everything you want to find out about
- ☑ Thank the learner for their contribution

As teachers, we can select evaluation methods that are appropriate for our learners, session or programme. We can choose between formal and informal methods of evaluation. It is helpful if you can use a range of techniques to collect information about your programmes and evaluate their progress.

Activity 13.4

Which evaluation techniques would be suitable for your learners and your programme?

Returning to self-evaluation, it may now be useful to consider in more detail exactly what we might be taking into account in this process. Some teachers make their own checklist to use after each session. You will undoubtedly find it helpful to devise a checklist of your own which fits your own particular context. You may find it useful to consult the examples that follow on pages 196–97.

Action based on evaluation findings

So far we have looked at the first part of evaluation – gathering information. Next we will consider how we might put this information to use in improving our teaching.

There is no point in evaluating a session or programme unless we follow up the results of the evaluation and plan for improvement. If things have gone well we will want to build on these; if things have not gone well we will want to consider changes to implement on future occasions.

This is where an action plan can be helpful. Its purpose is to:

- Ensure that we learn from the experience that we have had
- Establish priorities
- Identify responsibilities
- Establish the timescale within which changes should occur

In our action plan we would therefore specify what should be done, by whom and by when. An example is provided on page 198 which you can adapt to suit your professional situation.

Session Evaluation Form

During this session, what seemed to go well was:

I think this was because:

What didn't appear to go well was:

I think this was because:

If I repeat this session
I will do again:

I will change:

 Achieving Your PTLLS Award © Mary Francis and Jim Gould 2009

Checklist for evaluating a session

How effective was ...	Very effective	Effective	Satisfactory	Needs attention
Introduction to the session				
Making outcomes clear to learners				
Structure of the session				
Emphasis placed on key points				
Pacing				
Use of voice				
Level of interest maintained				
Use of questioning				
Balance of teacher/learner activity				
Motivating learners				
Level of participation				
Types of teaching materials				
Use of teaching materials				
Checking on learning				
Summarising and bringing session to an end				

Significant features of the session:

What will I do differently next time?

Action Planning

Issue	Change	By when?
Learners lost concentration after 45 minutes	Review activities and plan to increase active learning methods	Next session
Learners unable to perform skill	Re-do skills analysis and plan a spot demonstration of difficult section	Next skill session
Ran out of materials for practice session	Technician to order materials required two weeks ahead	Next month
Learners found it difficult to cope with simulated practice conducted in the training room	Re-plan so that practice and assessment takes place in the workplace	Before next course

Action plans can also provide a useful method of bringing sessions or programmes to a conclusion. In this context, we are talking about learners drawing up their own individual action plans. They are encouraged to summarise what they have learned and how they will put this to use in their own working environment.

This can be done informally or can be made more formal by learners filling in an individual action plan that they then take away with them. It may differ from the action planning example given above, as its function is rather different. A suggested layout for an individual action plan is given opposite.

If we refer back to the purpose of evaluation we can see that action planning completes the process of evaluation, as it takes us to the stage where 'We can then **use** this information **to improve** future sessions or programmes that we conduct'. Evaluation is as crucial to the planning process as is preparation and planning. If you refer back to the Planning Cycle in Chapter 4, you will see that evaluation brings us to the end of the cycle and informs our planning at the beginning of the next cycle.

So, it is important to evaluate the learning that takes place in our sessions and to draw up an action plan for how we might do things differently. At course or programme level a similar review is undertaken, drawing on the outcomes of evaluation, such as yours, together with statistics on the retention and achievement of learners.

It is critical that evaluation also takes place at an institutional level where, amongst other indicators, it will draw on the observations of staff teaching. Evaluation allows an institution, whether a college, a work-based learning provider or an adult education service, to take stock, produce a self-assessment report (SAR) and develop a quality improvement plan (QIP). These can then inform the direction of the institution through discussion with directors, governors and funding bodies and be used as part of the evidence base for an inspection.

Individual Action Plan

Name: ....   Date: ....   Session: ....

The five major points I have learned from this session are:

1

2

3

4

5

How I will use each of these to improve my practice:

Learning point	How I will use it	Target date	Completed
1			
2			
3			
4			
5			

I will review my progress on this action plan on .... (date)

Chapter summary

The main points covered in this chapter are:

- ✓ Assessment measures achievement of learners; evaluation measures the overall effectiveness of teaching sessions or courses
- ✓ Evaluation is an ongoing informal process
- ✓ Formal evaluations can be carried out using either spoken or written techniques
- ✓ Different discussion techniques can be used to make spoken evaluations more objective and representative
- ✓ Evaluation questionnaires can use a mixture of open and closed questions
- ✓ Evaluation should result in an action plan detailing changes to be implemented
- ✓ Evaluation takes place at all levels, ranging from self-evaluation of teaching sessions to full institutional evaluations of overall provision

Further reading

Tummons, J. (2007) *Assessing Learning in the Lifelong Learning Sector.* Exeter: Learning Matters. Although based around the evaluation of assessment processes, Chapter 8 in this book gives a clear and comprehensive coverage of all facets of evaluation, particularly those aspects concerning external bodies.

Hillier, Y. (2005) *Reflective Teaching in Further and Adult Education,* (2nd Edn). London: Continuum. Chapter 9 gives detailed coverage of evaluation, evaluation methods and how to deal with the results of evaluation.

Useful websites

For inspection guidance and reports
www.ofsted.gov.uk

Learning and Skills Improvement Service
www.lsis.org.uk

14

Microteaching

Chapter overview

When you have worked through this chapter on microteaching you will be able to:

- **Plan a microteaching session**
- **Develop strategies to deliver the teaching**
- **Justify your choice of methods, resources and room layout**
- **Recognise the importance of reflecting on practice in order to improve as a teacher**
- **Make the most of discussion and feedback after a session**
- **Develop a plan for your future development**

Microteaching explained

In order to gain the PTLLS award it is a requirement that your teaching is observed. This may be an observation of you teaching your own learners but it is more likely that you will be observed teaching a short extract from a session and the learners may be your peers from the PTLLS programme. This short extract is variously called peer group teaching, a 'mini lesson' or 'microteaching'. We will use the term 'microteaching' in this chapter.

Ultimately, as a teacher, you want your learners to be able to use what they have learned in a meaningful way. Similarly, that has been the aim of this book; the microteaching session will allow you to draw together all the knowledge you have gained from this book and test out whether you can put it into practice.

This chapter is intended to help you plan for your microteaching session and give you the maximum opportunity to demonstrate the effectiveness of your teaching skills. The planning techniques that you will need are those you have already covered in previous chapters, but we will now relate these to the more focused microteaching setting.

Planning for microteaching

As part of your PTLLS course, you are likely to be given guidance on the microteaching task. The guidance will probably stipulate:

- Length of time for the microteaching
- Where it will be held
- The resources that will be available
- Arrangements/roles for observation and participation
- Planning and documentation requirements
- Guidance on self and peer evaluation

And may look something like this:

1 Devise a learning objective that can be achieved in 30 minutes
2 Select appropriate learning activity(ies)
3 Bring any learning resources for a class of 12 learners
4 Bring the plan for the session with you
5 Be prepared to discuss your teaching with the group afterwards

On pages 203–4 you will see a blank plan suitable for a microteaching session. We suggest that you photocopy this form and fill in the sections on the plan for your microteaching session as you work through this chapter. The numbers in brackets suggest the order of completion.

Activity 14.1

Fill in the general details about your microteaching – who, where and when – in boxes labelled 1 on the microteaching plan.

You will now want to think about the group you will teach. What will you know in advance about your learners? What kind of learners are they? What do they already know? Later you can use this information to exploit the diversity in the group and plan for differentiation.

Activity 14.2

Fill in box 2 on the microteaching plan.

Microteaching plan

Course: [1]		Group: [1]
Venue: [1]	Time: [1]	Date: [1]
Topic/Title: [3]		Aim: [3]

Learning outcomes: [3]	How each outcome will be assessed: [6]	Checklist of resources required: [5]

Notes on learners: [2]	Differentiation strategies: [7]	Links to functional skills: [7]

Self-evaluation: [9]

Time [8]	Development [4]	Delivery [4]		Resources [5]	Assessment [6]
		Teacher activity	Learner activity		
	Introduction				
	Middle				
	End				

Next you will be thinking about what new learning you could introduce to this group. If you do not have experience of teaching it is probably best to select a topic that you are already confident about and therefore comfortable with. If you already have experience then this is a good time to select something new or to try out a specific activity or assessment method. Whichever the case may be, you need to arrive at a topic that will have some relevance and interest for the group you have identified above.

It is advisable to choose a topic that allows the group to be 'themselves' rather than to imagine they are someone else. If you were going to conduct a session on functional skills, for instance, you need to find a topic that is suitable for the group rather than asking them to imagine they cannot spell or are limited in their reading skills.

What objective will you set? Hopefully you will remember that a well-written objective will be SMART (if you need to refresh your memory on this, refer back to the section on objective writing in Chapter 4). The focus should be on your learners, 'At the end of the session each **learner** will be able to ...'.

For many new teachers the biggest pitfall in selecting learning objectives for microteaching is to be over-ambitious for the time allocated. This can result in you, the teacher, getting though your material, but none of your learners doing so! So think carefully, from the perspective of your learners, about what they will be able to achieve in the available time.

Activity 14.3

Write your topic, aim and learning objectives in boxes labelled 3 on the microteaching plan.

What kind of objective have you written? Does it involve your learners achieving knowledge, skills or attitudes? What activities will be suitable for this type of objective? Next consider how you will develop your content, what 'must' learners know? In Chapter 6 we focused on promoting 'active learning'; now think carefully about how varying activities will be of benefit to learners; a mix of 'you do', 'they do' works well. Remember that you may need to allocate time for switching from one activity to another, particularly if it involves learners moving.

And do not forget that the session needs a beginning, middle and end!

Activity 14.4

Fill in the development and 'delivery' columns, both labelled 4 on the microteaching plan.

What resources will aid learning? In a short session it is best to have few and simple resources. Some form of visual aid or 'the real thing' (see Chapter 9) to highlight the main points in the 'you do' part of the session, and perhaps a handout with instructions or gaps to fill for the 'they do' part will probably suffice. Remember to exploit whatever you use to its best advantage.

 Activity 14.5

Fill in the resources column and resources checklist box, both labelled 5 on the microteaching plan.

The next stage is to think about how you will assess what your learners have achieved. If you have written a SMART objective at the beginning then you will have a clear idea about how to assess whether or not learners have achieved it. If you are struggling with this perhaps you need to have another look at your objective. You may be able to include some short quiz or test at the end of the session but if time is short you may well be more likely to opt for a more informal approach that fits easily with the planned delivery of the session. Chapter 10 will remind you of some possible approaches.

Activity 14.6

Fill in the assessment method(s) in box 6 on the microteaching plan.

The next thing you will want to feel confident about is that you have planned to be inclusive in this microteaching. Are there any individual needs or experiences that you need to be aware of and plan for? In a short session, such as this, it is less likely that you will be able to develop functional skills but are there any particular functional skills that will be required in order for learners to achieve the objective?

Activity 14.7

Fill in the sections on differentiation and functional skills in boxes both labelled 7 on the microteaching plan.

Managing timing can be more difficult in a microteaching session than it might be in an actual teaching session. Because of the relatively short length of time involved in the microteaching, there is less room for manoeuvre, particularly if you are planning any exercise that is learner-led. The likelihood is that you will run out of time, rather than finish early, so you need to include a few time checks on your plan so that you can pace yourself appropriately.

 Activity 14.8

Fill in the timing in box 8 on the microteaching plan.

You should now have completed all the sections on your plan, except the box labelled 9, self-evaluation, because that occurs after the session.

There are a lot of small steps here, but following this process will enable you to plan logically for teaching and learning. Now the last step, check your plan against the items below:

Checklist for microteaching lesson plan

☑ Is the topic suitable for this group?

☑ Have I ensured that everyone will feel included and part of the session?

☑ Have I considered functional skills?

☑ Are the objectives SMART?

☑ Can the objectives really be achieved in the time allocated?

☑ Do I have a mix of activity with an appropriate balance of 'you do' and 'they do'?

☑ Have I planned to make best use of my resources and will there be any problems concerning availability?

☑ Have I included some form of assessment in my plan?

☑ Do I have a clear structure that includes a beginning, middle and end?

☑ Have I considered the 'reality factor'? Will what I have planned actually work in my setting?

Being positive about microteaching

You should now have as near perfect a plan as you can make it. However, how well you do in microteaching will not just be about planning or teaching knowledge or teaching skills; the attitudes that you bring to the classroom will also influence the outcome. As we discussed in Chapter 3, it is much easier to relate to learners:

- If you hold them in a positive regard
- If you are relaxed

If you have not taught before remember the audience is friendly and wants you to succeed. If you have picked a topic you are comfortable with you should not feel a need to rush or to be afraid of silences.

We are all different and can gain confidence in different ways. What might help you achieve a relaxed and positive approach to your teaching?

Activity 14.9

Jot down anything that you know helps you to be more relaxed:

Here are some ideas from previous learners/microteachers:

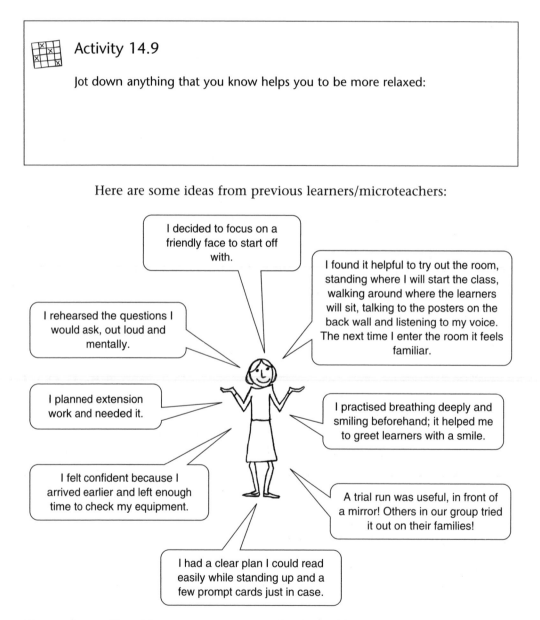

I decided to focus on a friendly face to start off with.

I found it helpful to try out the room, standing where I will start the class, walking around where the learners will sit, talking to the posters on the back wall and listening to my voice. The next time I enter the room it feels familiar.

I rehearsed the questions I would ask, out loud and mentally.

I planned extension work and needed it.

I practised breathing deeply and smiling beforehand; it helped me to greet learners with a smile.

I felt confident because I arrived earlier and left enough time to check my equipment.

A trial run was useful, in front of a mirror! Others in our group tried it out on their families!

I had a clear plan I could read easily while standing up and a few prompt cards just in case.

If you plan well and have a positive attitude, this is likely to lead you to a successful microteaching experience.

Delivering the session

In previous chapters you have worked through various aspects that you will now be able to use in delivering your microteaching.

- The beginning will set the tone; when you start, aim for eye contact to involve all your learners (for more on this see Chapter 2).
- Communicate the objectives early on and ensure instructions and explanations are clearly communicated (for more on this see Chapter 2).
- Signal clearly to learners when you move from one activity to another and make sure your session has an obvious beginning, middle and end (for more on this see Chapter 12).
- Treat learners fairly and as individuals. Make sure that you involve them all; use questions where pertinent, listening and responding appropriately. Encourage learners and give praise for contributions (for more on this see Chapters 5, 6 and 10).
- Pace your microteaching to fit the times on your session plan but remember that flexibility is also important (for more on this see Chapter 12).
- Exploit your learning resources (for more on this see Chapter 9).
- Review the session at the end – 'So, what have we learnt?' – and thank learners for their participation (for more on this see Chapter 13).

After the microteaching session

It is vital that you learn from your experience of teaching if you are to progress. You don't necessarily become a better teacher just by doing more and more teaching; experience that is not subjected to thought afterwards may mean repeating mistakes rather than improving. Good teachers become good by learning from their experience and by engaging in a process of self-evaluation.

We have discussed self-evaluation in the previous chapter. The microteaching experience provides additional opportunities for evaluation through discussion with your tutor and peer group after your session. It is likely that you will also be asked to contribute to discussion about the microteaching sessions of others who are on your PTLLS course. The purpose of this discussion is to develop your and their teaching rather than finding fault.

So how can you benefit and learn from the microteaching experience? The process of self-evaluation is intended to lead to improved practice; let us consider a sequence that could achieve this.

1 Teach the session.
2 Re-run the session in your mind, asking questions such as:

- What were the significant features?
- What went particularly well? What was I pleased with?
- What did not go as well as I had hoped it would?
- Did anything surprising happen?

3 Analyse the events you identified above and ask, 'Why did that happen?' Engaging in discussion about the 'Why?' forms a very useful part of the post microteaching discussion.
4 The results of this analysis will lead you to some conclusions about how you might do things differently and hopefully more effectively next time.

If you are an observer of microteaching you will also be asking these questions and engaging in reflection.

This cycle of learning is drawn from Kolb (1984). We have represented it in Figure 14.1.

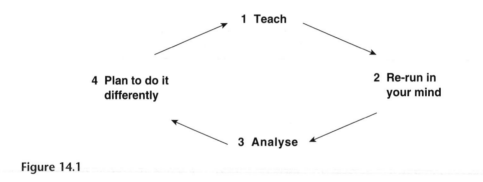

Figure 14.1

Kolb maintains that we learn through experience but only if we process that experience and make sense of it.

During the microteaching experience you will learn through observing others and giving feedback to them, as well as being observed yourself and receiving feedback from your tutor or group. It is useful to think about the way in which this feedback is given (see Chapter 7) so that you can provide feedback more effectively to others in your group.

Try to focus on:

- Acknowledging success
- Identifying strengths
- Identifying an area to develop for a future session
- Ideas for improvement

Ideas for improvement can then be built into an action plan, as we saw in the previous chapter.

After PTLLS

Once you have successfully completed your PTLLS course you can continue to develop your teaching through further professional development, particularly if it is well planned. By professional development we mean a process of continual appraisal and updating of the skills, knowledge and understanding relating to the teaching of your subject.

Your development plan should include both a focus on developing your teaching and on updating your subject specialism. You may well already have ideas about how you can take this forward. Have you considered the following?

☑ Reflect – undertake regular self-evaluation

☑ Ask your learners

☑ Watch someone teach

☑ Arrange to visit an 'expert'

☑ Go on a course or conference

☑ Visit another organisation similar to yours

☑ Search the net for the latest developments in your subject

☑ Ask someone to observe you

☑ Keep a learning log or journal

☑ Continue to read about teaching and learning

☑ Consider career advice, for example that offered by the University and College Union

☑ Update your subject specialism through professional journals and work experience

Where next?

Now that you may well be nearing successful completion of your PTLLS award your thoughts could be turning to the next stage in achieving QTLS and to registering with the Institute for Learning (IfL). The requirements of both are signposted in the references below.

We trust that working through this book will have prepared you to teach in the lifelong learning sector. It will also have given you a foundation for your future development and begun to introduce you to theory, such as that of Kolb, above, and ideas on how to cite and reference (see Appendix 3) that you will meet again at the next stage. We wish you the best of luck in your future professional life.

→ References

Kolb, D. (1984) *Experiential Learning: Experience as the Source of Learning and Development.* Upper Saddle River, NJ: Prentice Hall.

 Further reading

Hillier, Y. (2005) *Reflective Teaching in Further Education and Adult Education,* (2nd Edn). London: Continuum.
Contains useful ideas for continuing professional development

 Useful websites

Institute for Learning

www.ifl.ac.uk

Lifelong Learning UK

www.lluk.org

University and College Union

www.ucu.org.uk

UCU offers a range of professional resources and free membership whilst a student is training to teach in the lifelong learning sector.

For more on 14–19

www..dcsf.gov.uk/14–19

For more on Apprenticeships

www.apprenticeships.org.uk

For more on Adult Learning and Skills

www.dius.gov.uk

www.niace.

www.lsc.gov.uk

Appendix 1

Mapping the content of this book against PTLLS Qualification criteria

PTLLS Assessment Criteria		Chapter
1	UNDERSTAND OWN ROLE AND RESPONSIBILITIES AND BOUNDARIES OF ROLE IN RELATION TO TEACHING	
1.1	Review own role and responsibilities, and boundaries of own role as teacher	1
1.2	Summarise key aspects of relevant legislative requirements and codes of practice within a specific context	1
1.3	Review other points of referral available to meet the potential needs of learners	1
1.4	Discuss issues of equality and diversity, and ways to promote inclusion	5
1.5	Justify the need for record keeping	1 10 13
2	UNDERSTAND APPROPRIATE TEACHING AND LEARNING APPROACHES IN THE SPECIALIST AREA	
2.1	Identify, adopt and use relevant approaches to teaching and learning in relation to the specialist area	6 7 8
2.2	Evaluate a range of ways to embed elements of functional skills in the specialist area	11
2.3	Evaluate the teaching and learning approaches for a specific session	13

PTLLS Assessment Criteria	Chapter
3 DEMONSTRATE SESSION PLANNING SKILLS	
3.1 Plan a teaching and learning session which meets the needs of individual learners	4 5 12 14
3.2 Evaluate how the planned session meets the needs of individual learners	5 13
3.3 Analyse the effectiveness of resources for a specific session	9 13
4 UNDERSTAND HOW TO DELIVER INCLUSIVE SESSIONS WHICH MOTIVATE LEARNERS	
4.1 Analyse different ways to establish ground rules with learners which underpin appropriate behaviour and respect for others	2 3
4.2 Use a range of appropriate and effective teaching and learning approaches to engage and motivate learners	3 6 7 8
4.3 Explain different methods of giving feedback	8 10
4.4 Demonstrate good practice in giving feedback	8 10
4.5 Communicate appropriately and effectively with learners	2
4.6 Reflect on and evaluate the effectiveness of own teaching, making recommendations for modification as appropriate	13 14
5 UNDERSTAND THE USE OF DIFFERENT ASSESSMENT METHODS AND THE NEED FOR RECORD KEEPING	
5.1 Review a range of different assessment methods	10
5.2 Evaluate the use of assessment methods in different contexts, including reference to initial assessment	10 13
5.3 Justify the need for record keeping in relation to assessment	10

Appendix 2   Example session plan
Group plan

Group: AAT Foundation/Certificate	Venue: Room Q3	Time: 17:45 – 21:15	Date: 23/01/09
Topic/Title: Reports & Returns – VAT **Learning outcomes:** Each student will be able to: 1 Define VAT and how it works 2 Recognise the layout of a VAT return form 3 Correctly fill in a VAT return		**Aims:** To introduce the concepts, considerations and calculations for VAT	
		How each outcome will be assessed: 1 Written exercises 2 Results of groupwork 3 Peer marking exercise	**Checklist of resources required:** SmartBoard tools PowerPoint pres. no. 6 Gapped handout: 'VAT returns'
Notes on learners: 17 adults (19 years upwards) – wide age range. 30% male – 70% female 11 NVQ – 6 Diploma One Diploma student only started this term One NVQ student transferred from another class only last week There are four students for whom English is not the first language One student is dyslexic One student has mobility problems	**Differentiation strategies:** Mix of activity – explanation (aural), PowerPoint & Smartboard (visual), practical exercises (kinaesthetic) As there are a lot of 'little' parts of this topic, I am just putting one 'graduated' exercise of each type within the main body of the text so that the class can all progress through the material at the same rate but at their own level. The longer exercises at the end will be completed by the more able students, giving one-to-one time for those who grasp this less quickly Clarity of speech and straightforward use of English to help ESOL students Explanation of unusual vocabulary Handouts of a suitable font, size and colour for dyslexic student	**Links to functional skills:** Competence in basic Maths and English is expected. Those following the NVQ route are also likely to have been employed in this sector. All except the January starter have completed the 'Bookkeeping to Initial Trial Balance' part of the course Literacy – reading and comprehension of official forms Numeracy – simple mathematical operations (addition, subtraction, multiplication, division, calculation of percentages) ICT – volunteers will make contributions on the electronic whiteboard	

Self evaluation:

Overall, I was quite pleased with the way this session went. The introduction at the start enabled the newer students to feel part of the group; everyone took part and remained involved and responsive throughout the evening. The SmartBoard was useful for the presentation and helped to maintain attention. Most of the group came and used it to make a contribution. This was quite time-consuming – took longer than I had anticipated but I feel it was a worthwhile exercise for its positive effects on the dynamic of the group. The graded exercises worked well – most seemed to be working at a level which provided a challenge and I had some time to spend with those who needed help. I will use this approach again. The peer marking exercise was OK but could have been taken more seriously – became a bit too 'sociable'. Perhaps next time I will mix the pairs up instead of letting them work in the pairs where they always sit.

Time	Development	Delivery		Resources	Assessment
		Teacher activity	Learner activity		
Intro	Initial admin.	Explanation	Listen – chance to ask questions	Register	
17:45 –	Arrangements for next few weeks				
17:50	Recap of last week's session	Directed questioning	Answers		Q&A
Devel	**What is VAT and how does it work?**	Background, explanation of basic principles	Listen, ask questions	PowerPoint slides 1–4	
17:50– 18:05					
18:05– 18:15	Input and Output tax	Explanation	Questions – Complete exercise 1	PowerPoint slides 5–9. Gapped handout	Q&A Exercise results
18:15– 18:30	Invoicing	Information and example	Volunteers to fill in gaps on Smartboard	Smartboard	Contributions and questioning
18:30– 18:45	Imports and Exports	Explanation	List EU countries Exercise 2 (pairwork)	Gapped handout	Q&A Monitoring/ observation

Time	Development	Delivery		Resources	Assessment
		Teacher activity	Learner activity		
18:45 – 19:00			BREAK		
19:00 – 19:30	The VAT return	Describe boxes	Complete example return (small groups)	SmartBoard Returns exercise	Group feedback
19:30 – 20:00	Records, VAT control, errors and special schemes	Explanation of details		PowerPoint, slides 10 &11 Internet Smartboard Gapped handout	Q&A
20:00 – 20:45	Practice	Supervision and support as required	Listen, ask questions, make notes as required Try graduated examples (pairwork)		Observation
20:45 – 20:55	Feedback on answers	Give answers, respond to questions	Peer marking between pairs		Peer marking and questioning
End 20:55 – 21:00	Conclusion	Summary, next week's topic and reminder of arrangements			

Workshop plan

Course: First Diploma in Media	Module: Video Production	Venue: Studio 2
Learner 1		
Date: 09/06/08	Date: 16/06/08	Date: 23/06/08
Outcome/Target: To complete filming of drama. Film multiple takes and monitor sound through the use of headphones	**Outcome/Target**: To capture video footage onto Premiere Pro and make rough edit participating as part of a group	**Outcome/Target**: To complete rough edit and create an audio track using music and sound effects
Resource requirements: Filming kit, DV tape	**Resource requirements**: Premiere Pro workstation, DV tape	**Resource requirements**: Premiere Pro workstation, CDs, MP3 etc. of audio files
Progress/Evaluation: A wide range of shots filmed and sound monitored effectively. The whole script has now been filmed so editing can begin next lesson	**Progress/Evaluation**: Contributed well to group work and has assisted in editing at least two minutes of video in a logical order. Collect various audio tracks to insert in film by next week	**Progress/Evaluation**: Audio tracks used to good effect to create a tense atmosphere in the edited film. Next week, insert a title sequence and touch up effects/transitions to make the edits flow
Learner 2		
	Outcome/Target: Begin filming drama with careful reference to shooting schedule and storyboards. Aim to film at least two scenes with multiple takes	**Outcome/Target**: Complete filming of drama by reshooting conversation scene (with a tripod) and final scene.
Outcome/Target: Pre-production work – treatment and shooting. Schedule must be written, printed off and handed in	**Resource requirements**: Pre-production work for reference, filming kit and DV tape	**Resource requirements**: Filming kit, DV tape
Resource requirements: PC with printing facilities. Examples of pre-production forms		

(Continued)

(Continued)

Course: First Diploma in Media		Module: Video Production	Venue: Studio 2
	Date: 09/06/08	Date: 16/06/08	Date: 23/06/08
	Progress/Evaluation: Treatment and shooting schedule completed and handed work in. Possible improvements which can be made to improve grade suggested	Progress/Evaluation: Both planned scenes filmed and had time to film additional cut-away shots. Some of the shots are not steady so may need to be re-shot depending on time restraints	Progress/Evaluation: Footage is well filmed with good use of natural lighting and sound. Ready to begin editing next week
Learner 3	Outcome/Target: To use effects and transitions on edited drama to create excitement and tension	Outcome/Target: To adjust audio levels on edited drama and insert titles. Burn film onto DVD	Outcome/Target: Improve pre-production work following advice from formative assessment feedback
	Resource requirements: Premiere Pro workstation	Resource requirements: Premiere Pro workstation, recordable DVD	Resource requirements: PC with printing facilities. Previous work with formative feedback sheets
	Progress/Evaluation: Worked very well in producing an exciting drama which delivers a strong coherent meaning. Editing skills are of a very high standard	Progress/Evaluation: Drama completed to a near professional standard and work put onto DVD	Progress/Evaluation: Pre-production work improved following the given advice. Now begin preparation for the oral presentation next lesson

Course: First Diploma in Media	Module: Video Production	Venue: Studio 2
	Date: 09/06/08	Date: 16/06/08	Date: 23/06/08
Learner 4	**Outcome/Target:** Pre-production work – proposal and storyboards must be completed, printed off and handed in	**Outcome/Target:** Begin filming drama with careful use of camera work. Aim of filming introduction and main character's action scene	**Outcome/Target:** To capture video footage onto Premiere Pro and make rough edit of a minimum duration of two minutes
	Resources requirements: PC with printing facilities, storyboards sheets and pencils, examples of pre-production forms	**Resource requirements:** Pre-production work for reference, filming kit and DV tape	**Resource requirements:** Premiere Pro workstation, DV tape
	Progress/Evaluation: Completed proposal and storyboards and handed work in. Both pieces of work although late are of a good quality and do not need to be improved	**Progress/Evaluation:** All of the drama filmed to a good standard and ready to begin editing next lesson	**Progress/Evaluation:** Only one minute's worth of edited material due to problems with the Premiere Pro workstation. Continue with the editing before the next timetabled lesson

Appendix 3

Citing and referencing guidelines

When you write assignments for your PTLLS course, you will be drawing on:

- The content of the PTLLS sessions
- Your own experience and ideas
- The ideas expressed by others in books and other sources

We are providing this appendix to help you with the last of these three. How you acknowledge other people's contributions is an essential process if you wish to achieve the PTLLS award at Level 4 or progress to QTLS.

All assignments written at this level use other people's thoughts and ideas. It is usual to build upon existing knowledge rather than reinvent the wheel each time you tackle an assignment. You are therefore expected to use other people's work to introduce new ideas or support your own arguments. Quotes are normally used when they:

- Sum something up in a novel but concise manner – *'statistics can be used in much the same way as a drunk uses a lamp-post: for support rather than illumination'*.
- Define a particular bit of terminology – defines a support *role as 'one which directly supports teaching and learning but for which teaching is not the main purpose'*.
- Directly support a point you want to make – also suggests that *'it is not easy to estimate how long an activity will take'*.

When you use a quote, you are expected to acknowledge this, identifying which parts of your assignment have been taken from someone else's book or article. When you do this you are **citing**!

When your tutor reads your assignment they may find your quote interesting and want to read more. You therefore have to give them sufficient information to allow them to track down the original piece of work from which you have quoted. This is **referencing**.

Let us take an example. You have to complete an assignment on negotiating ground rules for next week and have just found an appropriate quote to use which is:

Once the rules are established you may be able to bend them a bit, but be fair and consistent even then.

You found it on page 102 of a book called *Teaching Today*. This is the third edition of this book, which Geoff Petty wrote in 2004 and is published by Nelson Thornes. You want to include this in your assignment on ground rules. How do you go about citing and referencing?

To cite

You have to give the reader a signal that this is someone else's work. There are two ways in which we can do this:

1 Run the quote into the text, but surround it with quote marks, like this:

> … text text text text, 'Once the rules are established you may be able to bend them a bit, but be fair and consistent even here' Text text text text text …

This is the procedure for shorter quotes (less than 30 words).

2 If you have decided to use a longer quote, it tends to get lost in the text so separate it out from the main body of text by leaving a blank line before and after and indenting the quote.

> … text text text text text text:
>
> > Once the rules are established you may be able to bend them a bit, but be fair and consistent even here. As far as possible, there should be a similar approach to rules and regimes from all the teachers the students experience.
>
> Text text text text text …

This is the procedure for longer quotes (approximately 30 words or more).

Having signalled the quote we now have to indicate whose work it is. To include all of the information above at this stage disrupts the flow for the reader, so initially we only need to supply sufficient information to contextualise the quote. You therefore give the name of the author and the year of publication of the source book. If the quote is a 'direct lift' from the book, then you also need to supply the number of the page upon which the quote can be found. If you do not, the reader will have to scan through the whole book to find it. Fine if it is on page 1, but a bit frustrating if it is on page 659! If it is a theory or idea that is mentioned, the page number can be omitted as the reader will be able to track it down by using the Index of the book.

So, using the above examples, citing would look like this:

> … text text text, although Petty (2004: 102) says, 'Once the rules are established you may be able to bend them a bit, but be fair and consistent even here.' Text text text …

> Text text text text, as Petty (2004: 102) points out:
>
> > Once the rules are established you may be able to bend them a bit, but be fair and consistent even here. As far as possible, there should be a similar approach to rules and regimes from all the teachers the students experience.
>
> Text text text text …

Or

> Text text text text:
>
> > Once the rules are established you may be able to bend them a bit, but be fair and consistent even here. As far as possible, there should be a similar approach to rules and regimes from all the teachers the students experience.
> >
> > (Petty, 2004: 102)
>
> Text text text text …

So much for citing.

To reference

We are now looking to tell the reader how they can track down the quote. We have told them the author, the year of publication and the page number (if required). We now have to tell them the title and edition of the book and the publisher. You display this information at the end of the assignment under the title of 'Reference List' in the following sequence:

1 Author
2 Year (this links the author to the particular book we are using. It is possible that we may have quoted from more than one book from the same author. The year of publication links the quote to the specific book)

3 Title of book (normally underlined or italicised to make it stand out)
4 Edition of book (if not first edition)
5 Publisher and their location

In our example the entry on the Reference List would be as follows:

Petty, G. (2004) *Teaching Today*, (3rd Edn). Cheltenham: Nelson Thornes.

If you use a number of different sources, you would list these in your reference list in alphabetical order of the first author's name. There are further refinements to the system but this should get you started and, hopefully, feeling more confident about the process.

You may wish to reference material you have found on the Internet. If so, care should be taken to make sure that whatever you wish to quote comes from a credible source. Who is the author, what qualifications do they have, are they really an authority on this subject? Having satisfied yourself that your source is legitimate, you proceed in much the same way as with a book, citing the author (or perhaps organisation) and either the year of the article or the year in which it was placed on the Web. The reference should include the title of the article, the website address (URL) and the date you accessed the information. Web pages are often changed or modified which is why the date of access is required.

Useful websites

You will find the following websites useful in helping you to format your references.

www.neilstoolbox.com/bibliography-creator/
www.library.uq.edu.au/training/citation/harvard_5.pdf

Glossary of terms

Aim   A general statement outlining what the teacher hopes to achieve during the session or programme of learning

Active learning   Techniques that encourage learning through 'doing' and interacting with the material being learned

Assertion   Expressing yourself in a self-confident manner

Assessment   The process of measuring the achievement of learners; judgement is made as to whether learning objectives have been met or not

Assessment records   The documents used to record the outcome of an assessment; these could be:

- an organisational proforma or log such as a candidate record sheet
- a document provided by an outside agency such as an Awarding Body
- a personal log held by the tutor or learner

Awarding Body   An organisation that issues course documentation and certificates nationally accredited courses

Blended learning   A combination of different approaches to learning, usually including some form of e-learning, used to deliver a specific programme or part of a programme

Communication   The transfer of information, from one person to another, with the intention of bringing about a response

Consonance   A state of harmony or agreement among the components of an attitude

Diagnostic assessment   The assessment used to discover the relative strengths and weaknesses in a learner's work and determine future action

Differentiation   The strategies used by teachers to manage the learning environment in such a way that they cater for the full range of individual difference

Dissonance   Inconsistency between the components of an attitude

Diversity   The recognition of the uniqueness of each learner in a typical learning group

Embed   To incorporate something (functional skills) into a greater whole (subject specialism) so it becomes an integral part

Equality   To be subjected to fair treatment – the same as others, equivalence. Possessing the same rights and value equal to all others in a specific group

Evaluation   Gathering information to give a measure of the effectiveness of the session or programme that has been delivered. The teacher can then use this information to improve future sessions or programmes

Extrinsic   Acting upon the person but originating from the external environment

Feedback   The giving of information to a learner or teacher on their performance, allowing them to identify particular strengths to build upon or weaknesses to be improved upon

Formative assessment   An assessment is formative when it is undertaken to measure progress. Formative assessment results are used to inform future learning and give feedback on progress made

Functional skills   The core elements of English, Maths and ICT that provide an individual with the essential knowledge, skills and understanding that will enable them to operate confidently, effectively and independently in life and at work

Ground rules   An agreed code of behaviour within a learning group

Ice-breaker   An activity, normally used at the beginning of a session or programme of teaching, which encourages learners to communicate with each other. It is designed to break down the barriers that invariably exist when a group of people meet for the first time

Inclusion   The process of making learners feel that they are fully part of the learning and social environment

Induction   To introduce learners to their new environment and its procedures

Initial assessment   The process of identifying appropriate learning programmes for individual learners based on level, suitability and the possible need for additional learning support

Intrinsic   Stemming from inside the individual rather than from any external source

Learning objectives   A statement of what is to be learned; objectives are written in a manner that is specific, expressing learning in an active form that can be relatively easily measured and assessed

Learning styles   The particular way in which an individual prefers to learn; the preferred way in which learners take in and process the information received during teaching

Microteaching   A scaled-down teaching performance delivered to a small group of peers during a short time period and accompanied by reasonably detailed feedback

Motivation   The force or reason behind a particular action

Non-verbal communication   Any communication that does not involve the spoken word; this includes body language, facial expressions and noises

Ofsted   Responsible for inspecting care for young people and education and training for learners of all ages.

Personal action plan   A systematic method of identifying and recording the strategies to be employed by an individual learner, in achieving a given goal or goals within a specified time frame

Personalisation   The process of tailoring delivery of a programme to the individual needs or characteristics of the participating learners

Reliability   The consistency of measurement achieved in the use of an assessment method. The results of assessment can be considered **reliable** if the same candidate would achieve the same result for the assessment if it were taken on another occasion or with another teacher

Role   The functions assigned to and behaviours expected of an individual who is acting in a particular capacity

Self-concept   The mental image or perception that an individual has of themselves

Skills analysis   The break down of a skill into its component parts or sub-skills

Stereotype   A conventional, formulaic and oversimplified conception, opinion, or image of a specific group

Summative assessment   An assessment made to determine the final level of achievement; this is not necessarily at the end of a complete learning programme but could be at the end of a particular stage in it (for example, the end of a learning module on a specific subject which will not be assessed again)

Validity   The extent to which an assessment method measures what it is supposed to measure

Verifier   A person who checks the assessment practices of teachers to ensure consistency and maintain standards; an internal verifier (IV) normally works within one organisation; an external verifier (EV) works for an Awarding Body and verifies assessment practices normally across several centres

Vocational   Relating to training which is intended to prepare learners for an occupation

Useful website

www.lsc.gov.uk/jargonbuster

Initials explained

CTLLS   Certificate in Teaching in the Lifelong Learning Sector

DTLLS   Diploma in Teaching in the Lifelong Learning Sector

FE   Further Education

GCSE   General Certificate in Secondary Education

ICT   Information Communications Technology; using computers in a broad sense

IfL   Institute for Learning

LLUK   Lifelong Learning UK

LSC   Learning and Skills Council

NVQ   National Vocational Qualification

PTLLS   Preparing to Teach in the Lifelong Learning Sector

QTLS   Qualified Teacher – Learning and Skills

Index